OVERCOMING YOUR NERVES

Overcoming Common Problems

OVERCOMING YOUR NERVES

Dr Tony Lake
B.A. (Hons), Ph.D.

SHELDON PRESS
LONDON

First published in Great Britain in 1982, as *How to Cope with your Nerves*, by
Sheldon Press, SPCK, Marylebone Road, London NW1 4DU

Fifth impression 1989

Printed in Great Britain by
Richard Clay Ltd, Bungay, Suffolk

ISBN 0 85969 590 5

For Muriel

Contents

I

The Pattern of Breakdown

What exactly is a nervous breakdown? The problem in answering this question is that every breakdown seems to be unlike any other. Breakdowns are as different as the people who have them. Nevertheless certain generalizations can be made about the way breakdowns develop. One useful way of doing this is to describe the seven stages which most sufferers go through when they have a breakdown and recover from it. These stages apply just as much to the big, dramatic breakdown which is serious enough for the sufferer to have to spend time in hospital; to the very distressing emotional crises which many of us have without hospitalization; and, as we shall see, to the short, sharp attacks of breakdown which happen all round us every day but which usually pass unnoticed.

A common problem

The first stage of any breakdown begins with a problem which you have had before but coped with. This time, however, you find that you cannot cope the same way. It hardly seems to matter what the actual problem is—it can be worry about your job or about a person you are close to, anger about the way you have been treated by people with power over you or those you love, fear of serious physical illness, or of nuclear war. Almost anything which causes guilt, fear, anger, or worry can form the focus for the start of a breakdown. Little by little, or sometimes all at once, the problem gets out of control. You may feel, for example, that some days you cope with it completely, while on other occasions you find yourself totally pre-

I

occupied with it. This is the 'can't cope—can cope—can't cope' pattern. You find you are going up and down like a yo-yo, coping one day, failing the next, and then having a good day. As the problem gets out of hand, there are fewer and fewer good days, and more and more of the ones where you cannot cope. There is often a feeling also that whatever you do to try to solve the problem it simply makes matters worse. You cannot seem to win whatever you try. But you find yourself trying harder and harder nevertheless.

We don't talk anymore

At the end of the first stage the problem is noticeably out of control. By this time, something else has also started to happen which becomes more obvious as the second stage gets under way. This is a steady or dramatic breakdown in communication with other people. Suppose, for example, that the focus of the breakdown is worry about work, such as a fear of being unable to do your job satisfactorily. You find yourself increasingly isolated from colleagues. The more you worry, and the harder you try to put things right, the fewer people there are that you can talk to about the problem. If the focus is your husband or wife—as when trust begins to break down in a marriage and feelings of jealousy start to get out of proportion—then communication between you and your partner can often take on a nightmarish quality of total unreality. You stop saying what you think or feel, and begin to examine in minute detail in your head exactly what was meant by even the most innocent-sounding casual remark. If the focus is money, you find yourself going out of your way to avoid communicating with people who have money they might lend you, as well as those to whom you owe money.

This progressive breakdown in communication leaves you unable to ask for help. In the early stages you may ask for it, or get offered it, but find you cannot take it. Not having taken a person's advice makes it more difficult for you to ask that person again and, even if you do ask, he is likely to become increasingly impatient with you. So you stop asking. When people try to help without being asked, as they sometimes do, this only seems to make matters worse. Your isolation increases.

By the end of this phase in a breakdown, the victim has a problem which is already out of control, and nobody whom he can talk to about it. If you reach this stage you tend to feel that nobody really can understand, partly because you do not understand yourself, and partly because when you try to explain the whole thing, it seems ridiculous. Many people reach this stage and stay there for some time, by bottling up their feelings and hoping that the problem will somehow go away of its own accord. They convince themselves that everything will be alright, or that it is not their problem but somebody else's. Nevertheless the problem is building up inside them, and a deep sense of despair gathers around it. This tendency leads on into the next stage. Unable to talk about it with anybody else, the victim begins to experience failure of internal communication also.

Who am I?

When life is going fairly smoothly, we appear not to think very much about our internal system of communication. Because other people seem to like us, we are less inclined to question whether or not we like ourselves. We can act on most issues without deep thought, and if we feel strong emotions we tend to act the way we want, only questioning how we feel if things go wrong. But all this depends on our system of internal communication—the way we feel about ourselves, make judgements, think our thoughts, and keep our self-confidence intact. At the third stage of breakdown it can become impossible to think straight, not just about the problem, but about everything else. You find great difficulty in knowing how you feel. You can find yourself talking to yourself and making no sense at all. Your self-confidence can evaporate. You can become pre-occupied for days with basic questions about who you are and whether anybody really knows you or cares about you. As the stage develops you can find that even the simplest of questions challenges all your power of thought and feeling and defeats it.

People experience this third stage—breakdown in communication with the self—in many different ways. One way, for example, is to think of yourself as two different people—the one who has all your bad qualities, and the one with all the good bits. The two stop talking to one another, so that what one of them does is of no concern to the other. For example, a man who reached this stage and who worked in the accounts department of a large company began to defraud the company but also reported himself for doing it. When he did so, he talked about himself as 'Mr So-and-so', as if he himself was another person entirely.

Another breakdown victim who reached this stage worked in an international telephone exchange, and began to send telegrams all over the world to well-known political figures, warning them of plans for war which he 'knew for certain' had been made by the USSR. He used a code he could not understand himself so that when he sent them he would not be letting his 'evil' self into the secret, in case this side of him leaked the information to the press. Sometimes the 'bad' side becomes a kleptomaniac, and goes on shop-lifting sprees which the 'good' side is never told about. Sometimes the 'good' side experiences a religious revelation which destroys the 'bad' side for ever.

4

I hate myself

Breakdown in internal communication need not be this dramatic to be very damaging. A common feature of this stage is that you completely reject yourself without showing this to anybody on the outside. You simply come to the conclusion, logically and calmly, that you are totally unlikable, that for anybody to try to like you is a waste of their time and energy, and that the world would be a better place without you. There is no point in fighting this, nor in doing anything about it. It is simply a truth which you have to live with.

The most important aspect of any breakdown in self-communication is that you can now act in ways for which you no longer feel responsible. Because you cannot or will not communicate with yourself about all your actions, you begin to lose control over your own behaviour in a new way. This sets the scene for the fourth act. Your self-control finally gives way. Some people just give in—they stop eating, washing, talking, fail to get up from their bed one morning, close their eyes and refuse to open them, cower in a corner giving way to a fear which nobody else can understand, or, in some other manner suddenly stop being an ordinary person able to look after themselves and become a patient needing expert care. Others give themselves up to the rage that is boiling inside them. Later they may look back and say that 'something seemed to snap'. Their actions take on a violent and unpredictable character. They may smash up the furniture or their children or anybody who happens to be close enough. Dramatic and tragic cases of people who reach this stage and barricade themselves into a high building with a gun are common enough. Sometimes they have a child or a wife with them.

A cry for help

This fourth stage is known as the 'acute' stage. Often it is the phase of the illness when the victim obtains for the first time the help he has needed for years before. Often the help he gets is inadequate—too little, and too late. Always, however, when a person's self-control fails, the result is that other people take control over him instead, substituting other-control for self-control. In the case of big, dramatic breakdowns, this usually entails removing the victim to a place of safety for special treatment. He has to be protected from the consequences of his own actions. Because people in acute emotional crisis have to hand over their problem to somebody else for help, this stage is often described also as the 'cry for help' stage. The cry has been made many times before, but because it was always subjected to some form of self-control, the victim of the breakdown has never been able to match the drama of his cry to the seriousness of his crisis.

A taste of death

It is this final loss of control which most people fear when they are worried about having a breakdown. The acute stage is talked about in the most dramatic terms—going over the edge of a precipice, completely losing your reason, as if it were the final, deathly act which brought perpetual darkness and the ruin of all possible futures. Indeed it is a kind of death, for the acute stage marks the death of an unwanted self, and the start of a long struggle to construct a new and more acceptable personality. It is a taste of death in another way, too, for every breakdown is a major crisis in a person's desire to go on living. It cannot be said that they regain their old desire, since in so many cases there was none to regain.

Crawling from the wreckage

In many ways the next three stages of the illness are a mirror-image of the early stages—the same thing shown in reverse. During stages five and six, the damage done in stages two and three has to be repaired. These were the phases of the illness in which external and internal communication failed and was suspended. After a breakdown the victim has to learn to trust again—to trust himself and to trust others. Both go together. He needs to learn how to show his anger and his fear, and to get both back into proportion. Many kinds of therapeutic techniques are used to enable the patient in hospital to restore his faith in himself and to express feelings safely. A painting, for example, may be made and discussed so that hidden anger or fear can be shared out in the open. People may 'act out' their fear or anger and, with the right help, see what they are doing. Group therapy can show people that they are once more able to express ideas and feelings and communicate them to others. Drugs are often used to 'stabilize' the patient, that is to say, to suppress those parts of his behaviour which may harm him, embarrass other people, or do both these things. Deeply sedated patients behave like zombies. But gradually and with luck the patient begins to take back the control over his own behaviour which he found himself abdicating as the illness developed.

More luck than judgement

Recovery from severe breakdown still, unfortunately, depends more on luck than those with good judgement would prefer. Time heals more patients than do psychiatrists. Two possible explanations for this fact are worth noting. First, a breakdown takes many years to brew; it would be remarkable if the damage of a life-time could all be repaired in a few short weeks. Secondly, organized

7

hospital psychiatry is a formidably inexact and inconsistent affair. About the only matter on which those involved can reach agreement is that the patients are ill. Even the question of what is meant by illness is, where breakdowns are concerned, a matter of continuing dispute among those who have the care of the acutely ill.

'Cope—can't cope'

During the final stages of recovery, the 'cope—can't cope' stage often recurs. After an acute crisis people often seem to take two steps forward and one-and-a-half steps back. Sometimes the strongest motive they have for getting better appears to be a fear of having to go back into hospital, not because they will not be helped there, but because they dread the help they will be given. This can be seen partly as a repeat of the early stage, when if others tried to help it made matters worse. Eventually, however, most people seem to shake off this inability to fend for themselves. They decide that they really do want to live and to get well, and that they have to do this for themselves. Life becomes something they can enjoy. This is the final stage.

A puzzling illness

There can be no doubt that nervous breakdown is an extremely unpleasant illness. But it is also a puzzling illness, particularly for those who are not familiar with psychiatry. Most of us are used to the idea that illness can be caused by germs or viruses, and that treatment in such cases means helping the body to kill off or repel harmful invaders so that it can be normal once more. Nervous breakdown is puzzling because it does not fit into our generally accepted ideas about illness. As far as we know there are no germs involved, and there is nothing 'organic-

8

ally' or 'physically' wrong with the victim. If somebody has a nervous breakdown, in what way is he ill?

The answer is that people who have nervous breakdowns are behaviourally ill. That is to say, the way they behave as a result of the illness is painful and distressing to themselves and to those around them. Their feelings are affected so they cannot respond in a normal manner to the demands of everyday life, so they can also be described as emotionally ill.

It is often said that they are 'mentally' ill, that they have an illness of the 'mind'. This is misleading. Although 'mind' is a useful word when we discuss thoughts and feelings, there is no such single physical object as a 'mind' inside a person. Many of us grew up believing that up there in our head was a special organ called the mind just as we have a heart, liver, and kidneys in other parts of the body. Unfortunately, it is not as simple as this. If it were, then perhaps doctors would be able to operate on it to put it right when it went wrong, or bathe it with medicines to make it better. All we have up there is brain and nerves, not a special, separate organ called the mind.

The brain and nerves in the head are part of a complicated control system which exists throughout the body. What is so puzzling about nervous breakdown is that when somebody is even very seriously ill this system still appears to be perfectly healthy. Some of the naturally occurring chemicals in the brain may appear in greater than usual quantities, but the nerve fibres, brain tissue, and glands appear to be as efficient as they were before. Nevertheless the person is ill, and we know this because he keeps doing things which hurt himself and other people. Nor is there a sudden lack of intelligence. Clever people do not lose their cleverness when they have a breakdown—they have very clever breakdowns. Their ways of behaving oddly demonstrate how clever they are. As for the use of drugs in the treatment of emotional illness, they are not designed to 'cure' the mind, in the sense that a shot of penicillin, for example, might kill off bacteria and cure a diseased organ. They are intended to slow down or speed up the patient's reactions, so that his behaviour becomes as a whole more manageable for a time. They are an aid to treatment, not a treatment in themselves.

Consistent unhappiness

The only safe judgement we can make, therefore, is that somebody has a breakdown when he or she is consistently very unhappy—either terrified of something, or very angry, or both. As a result of this unhappiness the person concerned cannot cope with problems, so they get out of proportion. As the unhappiness increases it becomes more and more difficult for the victim to communicate with other people, and to prevent the unhappiness bursting out —either in fits of rage or angry withdrawal which frighten the people around him, or in bouts of uncontrollable weeping which the victim cannot adequately explain. This places an intolerable strain on the victim's relationships, and he is forced increasingly to try to deal with his unhappiness alone; his internal system of communication very often cannot cope with this task.

Identify the enemy

In any struggle, the first move is to identify the enemy. Where nervous breakdown is concerned, the enemy is not a germ or virus, nor is it some kind of inherited genetic defect handed down at conception from the parents of the victim. The enemy is unhappiness. To know how to avoid nervous breakdown we need to understand our own vulnerability to doses, both large and small, of unhappiness.

Most of us have been brought up to believe that a certain amount of unhappiness is good for us. The more you think about this the more absurd it seems. It is a philosophy which blinds us to a simple and important fact: every nervous breakdown is evidence of intolerable unhappiness, and, even more important, every moment of intolerable unhappiness is a kind of nervous breakdown. If you fail to prevent nervous breakdown in your own life, then you will experience many such moments, and they may all run together so that there is no relief from them.

2
Medium and Short-Term Breakdown

As with any other illness, the severity or otherwise of a breakdown is popularly measured in terms of whether or not somebody has to go into hospital, and if so, how long he stays there. We tend to think of an accident or an illness as not being 'serious' unless we have to see a doctor about it, miss a few weeks of work, or go into hospital. Of course, there is a sense in which all accidents or illnesses should be taken seriously. They could develop complications, or turn out to be worse than we thought at the time. It would be particularly mistaken to regard minor breakdowns as less than serious. First, the road to the psychiatric wards is paved with minor breakdowns which have become progressively worse. Secondly, we all learn first-aid techniques so we can doctor ourselves when we have minor accidents or catch the 'flu. But very few of us are able to recognize, let alone treat our own small attacks of nervous breakdown. It is safer to regard them all as something to be taken seriously. The difficulty is, how do we recognize a minor nervous breakdown?

We will begin by looking at examples of what might be called medium-term crisis, and go on from there to discuss the short, sharp crisis which is perhaps even more dangerous because it is the more frequently ignored.

Bereavement

Medium-term crisis usually belongs to one of two groups. The first of these groups consists of intolerable unhappiness arising from a clearly identifiable cause. An obvious example is bereavement. When you lose somebody you love it is natural to feel very unhappy for a long time afterwards. The death of a very close friend, or of a husband or wife can still come as a great shock, even when the person concerned has been ill for a long time, and death had been expected. Faced with this crisis many of us feel that we do not want to live any longer without the person who has died. We would prefer to stop living. Alongside this terrible feeling of loss we may also experience a deep sense of outrage—sometimes anger at the unfairness of life, and at times an all-consuming rage towards the people who appear to have let it happen. If there is any doubt in your mind that your loved one could have been saved by better or earlier treatment; or if you feel guilty in any way that you may have contributed towards the person's death; or if you were angry with the person when he or she died, then your grief can be even harder to accept. Above all it is difficult to communicate this anger, to get other people to recognize and respect it, and to show that they understand without making you feel patronized. To make a full recovery you need to be able to express all the anger and fear, whatever its cause, and however disproportionate it may seem to others. A need to stay dignified, or to avoid embarrassing other people can stop you from letting go, and you will spread the emotional crisis over a longer period.

Emotional crisis is expected of people who have lost somebody they love. Or at least it should be, though this is not always the case. You may find yourself friendless and unsupported at such moments. To be pregnant and lose your unborn child does not always result in support and understanding from its father or your own mother. If your child dies in infancy you may find yourself grieving alone, long after others think you are over the crisis. After a stillbirth a mother may be rushed into getting pregnant again far too soon, before she has fully accepted the death, before she really wants to face another birth, and in order to 'take her mind off' the dead baby. She may feel great pressure from other people to stop thinking about her lost child, never to mention the baby, and to 'get over it', or 'put it behind her', as if it never existed. Enraged and hurt by such an attitude, she becomes the only one who really cares, and buries the anger and grief deep inside her, to be nursed secretly as long as she lives. Sometimes her next baby becomes a substitute for the lost child, rather than a person in his or her own right.

Only if we can touch the very bottom of our grief and know somebody else understands can we face death, and decide to live on. Otherwise we will never quite accept life fully, and the tragedy of bereavement will poison not only our own future, but also that of the people closest to us. Not all of us can find somebody who understands and, unable to communicate, we can become trapped in a life of intolerable unhappiness brightened by only occasional periods of tolerable unhappiness.

Broken relationships

Intolerable unhappiness is just as likely to occur when a marriage breaks up, or a love affair comes to an end, as it is when somebody you love dies. You grieve for the relationship which has died. On the whole, however, people tend to be less sympathetic. The hardest time is not usually the moment of final separation, but the period during which you become aware that the relationship is effectively over. You may stay together, married, or still recognized by the rest of the world as partners, for a long time after this. When trust and love are no longer part of a relationship communication can become impossible. If you have nobody to talk to the risk of major breakdown is worse. Many people in this situation tell their doctor that they cannot sleep, have lost their appetite, feel depressed, cannot stop worrying, or feel suicidal. Sometimes the doctor will make time to listen and to show he understands. Sometimes he will ask no questions, but reach for the prescription pad and issue tranquillizers, anti-depressants, or sleeping tablets.

Life turns sour

Bereavement, the break-up of an important relationship, losing your job or being demoted, a business failure which plunges you into debts you cannot meet—all these are common causes of medium-term breakdown. Sometimes, however, both long and medium-term breakdowns happen without an obvious identifiable cause. Life just seems to go sour on you. You can think of no explanation to give to other people. You feel depressed or permanently angry. You may be accused of 'moodiness', of being emotionally unpredictable. Perhaps you find yourself spending most of your days and nights feeling lonely and rejected. Maybe you seem totally involved in work, as if nothing else existed, in a frantic effort to accomplish something you know you could do in half the time if you were not so tired. If other people try to talk to you about this or to offer help, you over-react either by apologizing profusely for your own existence, or by becoming very angry, or aloof.

Major nervous breakdown is recognizable because the sufferer gives way to his own fear or anger and is totally consumed by these feelings. Medium-term breakdown is easiest to identify in cases where there is a clearly related cause, such as bereavement. When there is no obvious cause, and where you know the cause but cannot get anyone to understand, you may well have a short-term nervous breakdown and not receive help. How can you recognize short-term breakdowns?

Short-term breakdowns

This is a particularly important question, because it affects so many of us. Relatively few people (about 20,000 a year in the UK) reach the stage where they have to be detained in hospital for their own good. You may personally feel that this is never likely to happen to you. Also, people by and large seem to cope with personal tragedy remarkably well. Nevertheless we live in a society where short-term nervous breakdown is so common that much of it is regarded as normal. The bulk of these breakdowns are not clearly related to a particular causative event. They consist of short, sharp attacks of over-reaction. At the time they take place, the victim is intolerably unhappy, and his behaviour is out of control.

There is only one real difference between minor breakdowns and the major ones which usually end up with hospitalization, and that is the length of time they last. Otherwise the short attack of emotional crisis is just as horrific as the long one. It also has its three build-up stages —loss of control over the problem, communication breakdown first externally, and then internally with the self— and it also has an acute stage, and the three recovery stages. The central crisis is similarly concerned with whether you want to go on living or not. If fear takes over, you just give in. If anger wins, you find that 'something seems to snap' and you go over the edge into uncontrollable rage. If you make a complete recovery then you find yourself accepting life in a new way. If your recovery is only partial, then the cause of this particular breakdown stays inside you and continues to fester into a new one some day soon.

3
Notting

The idea behind this book is that if we are to avoid the big breakdowns we first have to learn to live without the little ones. This does not mean never losing your temper, or never having a good weep. From time to time, most of us need to let off steam in such ways. When tension builds up inside us, outbursts like these act as a safety valve. It could be argued that they help us to put off a worse breakdown.

The problem is that while these ways of releasing tension work for a short time, they are no answer in the long term. If you are to avoid even the remotest danger of a breakdown you have to deal with the cause, not simply provide more safety valves. Breakdowns are caused by a build-up of intolerable unhappiness inside a person. You have a breakdown when no other way is open to you of dealing with this build-up. Putting off a breakdown is no way to avoid one, it merely delays the illness. For a long-term solution you have to stop the build-up of unhappiness itself. And before you can stop it, you have to understand it.

Tying the not

The reason why tension builds up inside people when they are unhappy is because of one particular kind of human behaviour. It is probably one of the most significant and universal of all behaviours, but as yet no commonly accepted, unambiguous word exists for it. The name I use for it is *notting*. A few examples will help you understand the term and how to use it, and then we can go on to look

17

at the part played by notting in short-term nervous break-down.

Notting means working at not-doing something. Suppose, for example, that you are on a bus or train when a stranger catches your eye. He leers at you, and you know instantly that if you appear to be too friendly, he will be a nuisance. At the same time, you do not wish to be rude. So what you do is to 'not-smile' at him. Your lips curl slightly, and you look at him briefly, but your smile tends to be rather wooden and stiff, because you are working at not-smiling, instead of smiling. You will probably also start not-looking at him. To do this you fix your eyes on something else, and control your head so that you will not catch sight of him by accident. In this instance, notting shows as not-smiling and not-looking. They are very different from not smiling, which is how we would describe a person who simply does not happen to be smiling, and from not looking, which can happen when you are not even aware of the other person.

Not-speaking

Notting can be done in thousands of ways. For example, when two people have quarrelled, they are often said to be not-speaking to one another. They are actively avoiding talking to one another. If two people are not speaking, this simply means they do not happen to be talking at this moment. But if they are not-speaking, then they are going out of their way to avoid communication. Suppose they happen to be in the same room, and one of them is talking. His antagonist will probably take no notice of the words. That is to say, he will not-notice them.

Other common examples of notting are not-referring to somebody, as when you are afraid the mention of somebody will upset the hearer. This often happens to a bereaved person; it seems suddenly as though the one who has died never existed, because so many acquaintances carefully not-refer to him. Or there is not-offering, as when a friend can help but carefully fails to suggest an obvious way of doing so. For example, a neighbour may not-offer to babysit, even though he or she knows you would like this, and has often done so in the past. Students can spend many weeks not-writing an essay; husbands can make not-putting up a shelf, or not-decorating a room last for months. A delicate subject of conversation, which people skate round is being not-discussed, and so on.

The cost of notting

What is happening inside a person when he is notting? The first point to note is that notting takes up a certain amount of energy. If you happen not to be looking at somebody, then you are spending no energy at all on him. But if you are not-looking at him, you are making an effort. Similarly, if somebody calls your name and you are so engrossed in something else that you do not hear, your muscles and nerves have done no work as a result of the other person's action. But if you are deliberately not-hearing, you have to spend energy on stopping yourself from reacting. You hear your name, but you use calories in your muscles to control the impulse to turn round and respond to the other person.

Some instances of notting cost a great deal of energy. Picture a person who cannot stand heights, but for some reason or other has no choice but to cross a high bridge. Getting across that bridge will cost him almost all the energy he has. When he reaches the other side he will probably be in a state of collapse. He has had to spend energy on not-looking down, on not-letting go of the rail, on not-being afraid, on not-going back, and so on. To people who do not understand, this may seem comical to watch, but to the person concerned it is very hard work.

Usually people who cannot stand heights go out of their way to not-cross bridges. That is to say, they use up a similar amount of energy going the long way round.

Anger and fear

The second point to note is that notting is almost always a response to anger or to fear. Thus, not-speaking with some somebody is usually the result of anger. Not-crossing the bridge was due to fear. When people talk about anger and fear, however, they do not always use these words. The language contains many different ways of describing these two emotions. A very small amount of anger, for example, can be referred to as irritation, or frustration, resistance or annoyance. A small amount of fear may be called mild anxiety, disquiet, or uneasiness. We are all capable of feeling anger or fear in many different ways, and to different degrees of intensity. They range from slight anger or fear to absolute rage or utter terror. If we look back at some of the earlier examples of notting, the connection will become clearer. Not-referring to somebody who has died, for instance, is done by people who are to some extent afraid of upsetting the bereaved person. The fear may be slight, but this is what causes the notting. The student who not-writes an essay is probably anxious. The friend who not-offers may be slightly irritated at being expected to offer—a form of anger. The husband who spends months not-putting up shelves may also be showing mild anger, perhaps because he would prefer to be treated more as a person in his own right and less as a stereotype husband.

What has all this to do with breakdowns? The connection is that when a person has a breakdown he is taken over either by anger or fear, or by a mixture of the two. These emotions are the basic causes of unhappiness. Anything which makes you angry or afraid causes you to be unhappy. If you are only slightly angry or afraid, then you will feel mildly unhappy. Extreme anger or fear is the reason for intolerable unhappiness—the sort which people experience during the acute stage of a breakdown.

It is because of notting that anger and fear can build up inside a person. This happens in such a way that tension is created within the muscles, and the person's nervous system is constantly on the alert preventing him from relaxing. We saw earlier that if we are to avoid nervous breakdown, we have to be able to stop the build-up of tension and unhappiness which takes place during the first three stages of the illness. The next step is to see what is happening to a person's body when he is notting in response to anger or fear.

A state of emergency

The effect upon the human body of anger and fear has been understood for many years. These emotions arise naturally when you are threatened. They trigger off a response by the autonomic nervous system. To deal with the threat, your body gets ready either for 'fight' or 'flight'. One part of the autonomic nervous system sets aside a certain amount of energy for emergency use all the time, and when the threat occurs, it begins to add to this store. Another part of the same system keeps the body in a state of emergency in case all the energy has to be used very quickly to deal with the threat.

The longer a person keeps on notting, the more energy has to be set aside for emergency use, and the longer his nerves are kept in a state of emergency. Tension builds up because the muscles are not allowed to use the calories they contain. All the time this is going on, of course, the reason for the anger or fear has not been dealt with. Notting means you are not-doing anything about the threat. So your body is faced with a double demand for energy: one lot because you continue to be threatened, and another lot to hold yourself in check and do nothing about the threat.

The burn-up

You can get an idea of how much energy can be stored up inside a person as a consequence of notting if you watch what happens when he eventually loses his temper. The pent up energy is released. The voice reaches its maximum volume. All the muscles are tightened and then relaxed, then tightened again very rapidly. Breathing is violent. The body becomes hot with this massive burn-up of energy. Gestures tend to be rapid and vigorous. The nervous system can no longer control what is happening through the conscious efforts of the person.

If you have watched somebody weeping uncontrollably, after spending a long time not-weeping, you will have seen a similar burn-up. Sometimes people weep with rage, but weeping like this can also be the result of desperate fear or misery.

In the same way you may have noticed that somebody who worries a great deal also spends considerable energy on what appear to be meaningless physical activities—wringing their hands, biting their lip, endlessly dusting and cleaning things, straightening objects on a table or desk top, and so on. These are known as 'displacement activities'. The best description of worry is that it is a combination of anger and fear. The energy required for keeping in all that pent-up emotion is so considerable that it appears to overflow; just as water drips over the side of the bath when it is too full, some of the energy is 'displaced'. A worried person can seem to be tightly packed with energy which he or she does not quite know how to control.

Notting is hard work

Notting is much harder work at some times than at others. This is because the amount of energy spent on notting is in direct proportion to the intensity of the anger or fear on which it is based. Thus the more angry you become with a person, the more energy gets stored up in not-speaking to him, or not-pleasing him, or even not-caring about him. The more afraid you are of somebody you have to live or work with, the more energy you need to force yourself to talk to that person without letting him know you are afraid. You cannot use this energy for anything positive, since it is earmarked for notting. The more notting you do, the harder it becomes to find spare energy for other activities. Life itself becomes hard work.

For example, suppose you feel like swearing at somebody, but realize that this might make the situation worse. You decide to not-swear. The energy which you want to spend on swearing stays in your muscles, ready to be used. You put slightly more energy into the same muscles to stop yourself swearing. You now have less energy to spare for somebody else. Let us now suppose that another person comes along who also does something to annoy you. Again, it might seem diplomatic not to express your annoyance, so once more you stop yourself from showing your anger—perhaps you decide to not-hit him, or to not-shout at him. Energy goes to the arm muscles ready to hit him, and even more energy has to be sent after it to hold the muscles in check. You have to do the same with your voice and breathing muscles, so as to not-shout. By now you have very little energy which is not already tied up. Any person who crosses your path from this point until you simmer down is going to find you very difficult to live with.

Problems, problems

Some people do more notting than others. This is because

they happen to be angrier or more afraid. Usually they have more to be afraid of or more to be angry about, although this may not be apparent to other people at the time. Often the causative anger and fear have arisen in earlier situations, and the person is still notting days, months, or years later. Unsolved problems from the past cause many breakdowns. The people with the most unsolved problems are the most likely to be so scared or so angry that they need to control themselves all the time.

We have already seen that the first stage of a breakdown focuses round a problem. Problems can be divided into two types according to the risk attached to failing to solve them. One type means that if you cannot find a solution you are not absolutely worse off than before, but have not managed to improve your way of life. It is as though a small gamble has failed. For example, you may be well paid, and try to get promoted. If you fail this is a problem, but you are not actually reduced in circumstances by the failure.

The second type of problem carries the risk that you will suffer a real loss, rather than a comparative loss. Losing your job and never being able to get another one is such a problem. The death of somebody you love is also this type of problem. The bigger the risk, the more likely you are to experience fear or anger. When the worst kind of personal tragedy happens, all the fear and anger which result can require so much energy that your body does not know how to obtain enough. There may not be sufficient in store to deal with the crisis. So, just to keep you alive, your automatic defences come into operation, and stop you feeling all the pain at once. This is the state known as shock. When this happens, you are prevented from feeling all the anger or fear. This too is a kind of notting. But people who are very badly hurt may continue to not-feel the pain long after other people think the state of shock has passed. Because the victim is not-feeling the pain he may also mistakenly think he is out of shock. When a similar problem occurs later, he is less able to deal with it because he still has not finally recovered from his earlier bad experience.

A history of notting

The first stage of a breakdown, then, is often connected with a long previous history of notting. So is the second stage. This is the point at which communication with other people begins to fail. Anger and fear result in a person not-speaking, not-listening, not-touching, and generally not-communicating. If internal communication also fails, and the third stage is reached, then the victim begins increasingly to not-feel his own fear or anger. It is as though he is in a permanent state of shock.

The crisis point in any breakdown is to do with whether you really want to go on living or not. Extreme rage means that you want to destroy yourself, somebody else, or the whole world. Extreme fear means that you desperately wish to escape even from your own body. In a breakdown crisis, whether it lasts for years or only for a few minutes, you are using up at a tremendous rate the energy which had earlier been stored up by notting. It is like a dam breaking under the pressure. Of course this can bring a temporary relief from tension. But in most short-term breakdowns the notting starts again once the victim feels better.

Notting leads to breakdowns; it also prevents people from making a full recovery from their breakdowns. The tension which was released during the acute stage is allowed to build up again. It is only if we can learn to stop notting that we can manage to live without these outbursts—however much they seem to help at the time. So it is important to understand all the implications of notting. Why is notting so destructive?

Investing in not-living

Whenever you are notting, you are investing energy in not-living. All the calories which are set aside and not used by even the simplest and most economical piece of notting are calories which henceforth will not be available for more pleasant activity. None of us can afford to waste energy. Notting is an energy investment plan designed to continue a policy of not-living. Also, it achieves nothing. Notting does not make the source of your anger or fear go away. It certainly does not make you feel better. It means you have to find a double quantity of energy just to do nothing. Why spend any time at all on not-living? Each moment you spend on notting is a moment of your present life destroyed and energy wasted which you need for the future.

Notting also means that you are angry about, or afraid of, the way your life is going, even though you may not want to admit this. Maybe you do not want to be treated just as a housewife or a husband, an employee or somebody's servant, a dutiful son or daughter, a faithful lover, or as an inferior person who is always expected to make somebody else feel superior. There are many ways in which people feel angry about how their lives have developed, and afraid also of the consequences should this anger get out. Notting can help them put off the day of judgement, when they have to make up their minds whether what they really want is to live another kind of life, or keep their way of life the same, as an unsatisfactory substitute. So notting can enable you to avoid life and death questions. When notting has to stop, and the breakdown crisis is upon you, you may find that nearly all the energy inside you is earmarked for notting. No wonder the crisis brings with it a feeling that you would be better off dead: you have no energy left to spare for living.

4
Looping

All nervous breakdowns centre around a crisis in a person's desire to go on living, or at least, the desire to go on with life the way it is at the time. In the case of minor breakdowns the crisis is temporary. With major ones it can last for years. The victims of breakdowns are reaping the harvest of having invested so much of their energy in not-living. When they cannot keep this up any longer the anger or fear spins out of control. Notting is a tendency we all have—an inability to face up to what is happening in our lives which frightens or angers us.

Loop the loop

Looping is another such tendency. This one gets its name from those railway systems which go round in a loop, such as the Circle Line on London's Underground. If you stay on to complete the ride you finish up exactly where you first started. Have you ever found yourself doing the same thing over and over again when you know you will end up being hurt every time? This is what loopers go through. They get stuck on a Circle Line in their lives and go round and round repeating exactly the same mistakes. At the end of each ride they find they have gone nowhere.

Notting and looping are closely connected. People who keep on making the same mistakes are refusing over and over again to do something more positive about their way of life. Each time they push away their feeling of un-happiness, and refuse to acknowledge it, they are taking a risk. Usually it is a risk which they have taken before, but this time they ignore all the evidence of past failure and believe that the circumstances are different. They never are.

Here I go again

Just as most of us are notters to some extent, so nearly every body is fitted up with behavioural loops. The most dramatic examples are the people who always seem to meet and to fall in love with the wrong kind of person, and always end up getting hurt. In a less obvious way nearly all of us have patterns of behaviour which can be triggered off by other people, and we end up failing to enjoy ourselves. 'I just knew it couldn't work,' we say, as we stand angry and amazed at our own ineptitude. 'Here I go again!' we think as we set off merrily repeating the same pattern a few weeks later.

The most tragic loopers are the addicts. Alcohol addicts cannot stop drinking. Once on the loop-line of a 'bender' there is no stopping them; they might as well stay on to the end of the ride. Drug addicts go round on their own ghost train. Work addicts climb aboard their own bandwagons, and suspend all the fun of life in order to end each day tired out and no fun to be with. Some loopers are compulsive gamblers, and not necessarily with the horses, dice, football pools, cards, or slot machines. You can be a compulsive gambler by wasting time and energy on lost causes—a job you know you hate, a marriage that cannot be saved, a violent partner who will never give up his contempt for himself or for you, but into whom you pour every small surplus of good feeling you ever accumulate, only to see it wasted every time.Compulsive gamblers prefer to lose, even though they know they are going round and round the same loop-line. Did you ever hear of one who could stop gambling while he was still ahead? Unless such people decide to give up their trip and enjoy the whole of life instead, nobody can help them.

Many of us have small loops which we go round with the help of special people who make us feel guilty. In effect the loop gives us a chance to over-react. A few examples will make this clearer.

A powerful mother

Karen is in her mid-thirties, married, and has three small children. She and her husband live on a new estate near her husband's work, while her mother, now a widow, lives about a day's travel away. Whenever Karen's mother is due to make a visit, Karen spends several days cleaning the house from top to bottom, even though she keeps it in perfect condition all the time. Karen knows she over-reacts whenever her mother announces a visit, and both Karen and her husband laugh about it. But she still feels the need to go round this loop. The fact is, her mother still has the power to make her feel guilty. Karen would not dream of telling her mother that behind this guilt lies fear and anger. She is afraid of her mother, and, at the same time, angry with her for making her scared.

Our kid

Bob and his wife, Julie, quarrel over their only son, Mark. Bob thinks his wife is 'too soft' with the boy.

Bob thinks Julie lets Mark get away with all manner of things without even a word of reproach—leaving food he has asked for, not putting away toys, criticizing his teachers and other adults, showing a general lack of respect for his parents. Bob says he would not have been allowed to do these things when he was little. Julie is determined to give her son a better childhood than her husband had. Almost every week Bob tries to explain how he wants the boy brought up, Julie argues, and Bob storms out of the house. Afterwards, Bob feels guilty and awkward, and tells him-self he is behaving like a clumsy fool. He would like to stop

29

repeating this pattern but does not know how to avoid going round the loop. What he cannot see is that by over-reacting to the situation he is able to treat himself the way his own father treated him—as a clumsy, awkward fool who could never be man enough. Bob and Julie enjoy kissing and making up after each argument. Julie has not told Bob that when he storms out feeling guilty, she is quite relieved to have him out of the house. She felt the same way about her own father. There was always more peace with him out of the house than when he was at home. Bob and Julie both have loops, and each has separate reasons for helping the other to over-react. They have given each other the power to make them feel guilty. Then each of them can suppress anger or fear out of a sense of guilt.

Naming the day

John is engaged to Diane. But he becomes angry whenever she tries to get him to fix a date for the wedding. He says he loves her, and he knows she loves him. He says he is not interested in marriage, that they could live together happily without all that fuss, and that this is what most couples do these days. Diane wants to live with John, but she would prefer to start as a wife, with a good house, nice neighbours, and real security. He seems contemptuous of this, so she does not mention it. Nor does she admit how much she would like to have a baby. Mentioning the wedding date helps her feel miserable about not being married even though she is past twenty-five, about not having a baby although most of her friends now have children, and helps her worry about whether John is really the right person for her, although she is convinced he is the best she can get. She also knows she can make John feel guilty about not marrying her, so she usually asks him about the date for the wedding just after they have had sex together. This makes John very angry, and then they can both feel bad—in her case, about having had sex without being married, and in John's case about not being ready to settle down. Their quarrels nearly always follow the same pattern. Sometimes, instead of the other way round, John will prompt Julie after they have made love, by asking when they are going to live together. She sulks and he gets angry.

Communication breakdown

Each of these three examples illustrates the little loops which 'happy', 'stable' people go through to obtain small, socially acceptable breakdowns. Communication breakdown plays a part in all nervous breakdowns, whether they are the mild or dramatic kind.

This breakdown in communication occurs first of all between yourself and other people. It shows as the feeling that somebody 'does not really understand'. Thus, Karen cannot really explain to her husband why she always reacts this way to news of her mother's impending visits. Nor can her husband adequately explain why he laughs. Also, Julie has not told Bob about the relief she feels when he storms out of the house. This is not simply relief caused by the argument; she would feel a similar sense of calmness if he went out without having the argument first. Diane and John both keep some important feelings to themselves also, such as Diane's wanting a baby, and John's uncertainty about settling down. Loops depend on feelings being kept hidden. The start of a loop is signalled by the feeling that the other person would not understand and that it is easier not to try to explain.

Caught in the loop

Whenever you go round a loop you also experience a loss of internal communication; you lose confidence in yourself, and you get the feeling that you are temporarily in the grip of forces you cannot control. This loss of self-control is important in two ways. First, it shows that other people's reactions are having an influence over you which is out of all proportion to the way you would like things to be. For example, Karen knows she is over-reacting to her mother, but she also feels helplessly caught up in this over-reaction. Bob too would like to stop going too far whenever he and his wife begin to quarrel, but it is as though something drives him without his consent. He says he cannot help himself. There is a feeling of inevitability—he feels forced to start shouting, and to escalate the conflict to the point where he slams the door and finds himself out on the street. Yet all the time part of him is fighting to avoid this sequence of events. And each time, this part of him loses the battle. Diane and John are no different in this respect. They too are caught up in a pattern they would like to escape from. Diane says that when the quarrel starts she often feels that she just cannot leave matters where they are. It is like having a spot on her face that she just has to pick at, even though she knows this will make it worse. She does not want John to influence her in this way, but cannot escape from the way she always seems to over-react. John too would like to be able to laugh when his girl-friend starts asking about wedding dates; he would prefer to be able to respond casually, but always finds himself putting a serious look on his face, blaming her, and feeling threatened.

Loss of self-control when you go round a loop means that the other person makes you feel bad despite the way you want to feel. But as well as this seemingly unavoidable need to over-react, there is also a tendency to punish yourself later for losing self-control. People who go round loops usually end up feeling ashamed, guilty, or stupid because of their over-reactions. They often show this by humbling themselves and apologizing profusely. When Karen hears that her mother is coming to see her, she stands awkwardly, grinning rather shyly, shifting her weight from one foot to the other, like a little girl who has been caught stealing sweets from the sweet jar. Her husband laughs at this point, and it is an affectionate laugh because this is the little girl he loves. But inside, Karen is angry with herself for not appearing self-assured and confident, and for not being grown up. As she cleans the already immaculate house she grumbles inside herself for doing work she knows is really unnecessary. But it is when her mother arrives that she feels worst of all. Her mother has a way of looking at the kitchen floor which strikes a chill into Karen's heart, however clean the floor is. All Karen can do is feel dumb with guilt.

Doing penance

After each quarrel about their son, both Bob and Julie feel very guilty and ashamed. They vie with one another to apologize the more profoundly. Each promises never to fight again. Bob feels stupid, and Julie tells herself to be a better wife and companion in future. They both do penance for having lost control. Bob brings his wife a cup of tea in bed, or does the washing up; Julie cooks Bob's favourite meal. They both make more of a fuss of their son. But within a few days this is over, and they settle back into their usual routine, and start working up to a new battle over the boy. With John and Diane, who are not yet married, the guilt-reaction following their fights is often shared with other people—Diane's sister, for example, and John's special friend at work. Diane shows how sad she feels and her sister comforts her by saying that she should be more patient. Things will work out in the long run; you have to give men time to settle down. Diane criticizes herself, and says she will never make a good wife, but her sister reassures her. In John's case it is his work-mate who provides reassurance. This takes the form of stories about how his own wife behaved before their marriage; John has to learn to expect women to be unpredictable and emotional, particularly after sex. It is all part of life's rich pattern, he says. But as long as you are getting it, you shouldn't grumble. At this point John usually grins and feels reassured.

When you go round a loop you find that each small breakdown in communication with somebody else contributes to a loss of self-control and self-confidence. It is as though you are collecting evidence of your own inadequacy, your own badness. When you have enough evidence, you give way to the feeling and the inevitable happens. You have a fit of temper, or over-react by feeling intolerably miserable, and as a result cause some small destructive episode to take place. You then complete the loop by trying to put matters right again—by apologizing, for example, or compensating for the damage you have done by some kind of penance. It is worth noting also that the misery you feel at the crisis stage is often reflected in physical symptoms at the reconciliation stage. Maybe you have a very bad headache, or your arms and shoulders ache. Many people experience back pain at this point. You carry on trying to put the relationship back together in spite of this.

Looping together

People who go round loops are very clever at finding the ideal companion, somebody who will help them to go round their loops. The two of them spin into orbit together. In the above examples, Karen's husband actually encourages her to over-react when his mother-in-law is due to visit. He likes the feeling that she is being kept on her toes by this old woman. It makes her into a better wife.

It also stops her becoming too clever in her own right, so he does not have to face his fear of being surpassed by his own wife. He prefers to think of her as an awkward little girl, rather than as a free and independent adult. He has enough competition to face at work, without wanting to compete at home. Sending her round her loop by laughing instead of talking the problem through enables him to go round a loop of his own. He can see it as her problem, nothing to do with his own emotions. He avoids his own fears, but also feels cross with himself, and makes it up to her later, by being more solicitous while mother-in-law is staying with them.

Using other people's loops to go round ones of your own is a normal part of relationships which are based on hidden unhappiness, and is called 'collusion', a term often used by psychiatrists and psychologists whose job it is to help people who have breakdowns. Bob and Julie collude so that each of them can go round loops which arose in the first place from their relationships with their parents. Bob was never man enough for his father; Julie loved her father but felt safer when he was out of the house. Diane and John are involved in loops with other people, her sister, and his work-mate.

Diane and John, Bob and Julie, Karen and her mother, Karen's husband and Karen—each of these relationships is helping the persons involved to suppress some degree of unhappiness at the way life is going. Most of the time it seems worthwhile to supress such feelings. Life, after all, is not completely unhappy. Perhaps most of us can expect to have to put up with moments of misery which well up from inside us and cannot be shared. By continually notting we get by in life; it is only to be expected, people say. So, by not-expressing the anger and fear which are causing unhappiness, and by finding somebody to share our life with who has similar hidden misery, we can keep our loops intact. The price we pay is that the loops take over from time to time, and we have short breakdowns. The advantage is that other people think we are happy. The disadvantage is that we remain unhappy, and set ourselves up for even bigger breakdowns later.

If you do a lot of notting, and have loops you would really like to get rid of, then your chances of even a minor breakdown are unacceptable by the best civilized standards. Although you may never experience a major breakdown, nevertheless you are spending more energy than you can afford on not-living. To the outside world you probably appear well-adjusted, able to cope with crisis, and in no danger of spinning out of control and having to be rescued by people in white coats. But inside you probably know the truth, that each time you go round a loop you are out of control, the victim of a pattern of behaviour which you will later punish yourself for not avoiding. Loops are really small breakdowns from which you fail to recover. If you want to, you can go on in this way till your turn comes to die. If not, then maybe it is time to change.

5
Reflex Training

We will assume at this point that there are patterns in your behaviour which you would like to change. For example, you may be aware of certain tendencies—loops you go round—which you know are destroying your chances of getting more out of life; or maybe you are aware that you often indulge in notting, and would like to stop. Habits like these can lead you into dangerous situations, or merely into short-lived episodes of intolerable unhappiness. Either way they are an investment in not-living. Giving them up will increase your safety from medium and long-term breakdown. How do you give them up?

The first step is to understand how they came to be there in the first place. There are general reasons for this, and there are particular reasons. The general ones are biological. That is to say, there is something in the make-up of every human being which enables him to develop behaviour patterns, both good and bad. We need to understand how and why people in general develop such patterns, and why some of these are more difficult to shake off than others. The next two chapters deal with this point. The particular reasons why you have your own set are laid down by your unique personality and experience of life. This question will be dealt with in a later chapter. First, another small excursion into the world of biological science.

Reflex actions

Consider a small conundrum. How is it that some people can put their hands in water which is not far off boiling, and other people cannot? Or how can some bathers enter a very hot bath with obvious signs of pleasure, whilst their nearest and dearest dip in one toe and shriek with genuine pain? The answer lies in the nature of what are called 'conditioned reflexes'.

A reflex action occurs whenever a person responds very quickly and without thinking consciously as a result of some kind of stimulus. The stimulus may be painful, as in the example of water which is too hot. If you put your hands in near-boiling water, you are likely to pull them out again very quickly without thinking about it because you respond directly to the pain. Some stimuli which lead to reflex actions are pleasurable. A person who is relaxed and mildly ticklish will probably respond to the stimulus of a feather under the chin by producing a complicated set of reflex actions which include pulling down the head, turning away from the feather, and laughing. Orgasm is, for the majority of human bodies, the most powerful of all pleasurable reflexes.

In the early days of scientific human biology it used to be thought that reflex actions could not be controlled, that they were automatic responses by the body triggered off by some external event. If the correct button was pushed the reflex appeared. The knee-jerk reflex is an example that most people will recognize, the doctor taps the patient's knee in the right place with a small rubber hammer, and unless there is something radically wrong, the patient's lower leg jerks upwards, much to the discomfort of inexperienced doctors who happen to be standing in the wrong place.

However, it is now widely recognized that a great many of the body's 'automatic' actions can be controlled. The reason why some people can put their hands in very hot water whilst others cannot is that the first group have learned or have been taught to control their reactions. The same reason explains also why some people are able to control their response to being tickled and why yet others have difficulty in experiencing orgasm.

Not-feeling

Control means not-feeling the stimulus. For example, the man who can stand very hot water puts up with the pain until he gets so used to it that he does not have to feel it any more. You can train yourself in the same way, by increasing the temperature little by little, and tolerating a little more pain each time. People can also learn to delay their response to pleasurable stimuli. Perhaps you can switch off your own ticklishness, or whilst making love, delay your own orgasm. It is all done by controlling feelings—by 'not-feeling'.

This human ability to delay pleasure and tolerate pain by notting is much more important than most of us realize. It is the basis of many things we regard as contributing to civilized life. For example, a courageous person is thought of as one who does not give in to fear but forces himself to complete a difficult and dangerous task. As we saw earlier, fear is the trigger for several reflexes, the need to run away, or to save yourself, and the reflexes which affect the internal workings of the body, causing it to tremble or sweat, or make the heart beat faster. 'Courage' means controlling these actions, or carrying on despite them. We tend to admire people who over-ride their own pain to do something courageous. Similarly we are taught to control greed, to wait for our pleasures until the appropriate time. It is often said that the world would be in a sorry state if everybody took what they wanted without considering the needs of others. Even simple, everyday politeness depends on putting off an immediate reward by investing energy in pleasing others first. To be a social success you are expected to be good at notting.

Whenever a person controls a reflex he has either to delay pleasure or tolerate a little pain or discomfort. You can train yourself to do this; but mostly you are taught by others. And the process begins at birth.

Teaching the children

When a baby is born it has no conscious brain with which it can control its own behaviour. That is to say, it is incapable of self-control. Its brain is almost entirely un-formed. But this does not mean a baby cannot produce a very wide selection of actions, as everybody who has met a new-born baby knows. The baby's body comes equipped with a large number of reflex actions. For example, if you pull faces at a very young baby it appears to pull faces back. If you stand it on its legs whilst supporting its weight it produces a series of walking actions. Many of its reflexes are complicated reactions rather like the loops we discussed earlier, in that if the reaction is triggered off when the correct 'button' is pressed, then a whole sequence of secondary reactions appear, always following the same pattern. For example, if the baby's face is stroked by a feeding bottle or the breast, then the baby turns its face towards the nipple until its lips touch the right place. It then opens its mouth. This reaction leads to another, for once the nipple is in the baby's mouth, a sucking reaction appears. The sucking triggers off in turn a swallowing reaction. The fact that these last two are connected is easy to demonstrate—simply find a very young baby, start feed-ing it, and then take the nipple or teat away. The swallow-ing stops as soon as the sucking, even if the baby's mouth is full of milk, and the unswallowed milk dribbles out.

Although a new-born baby can only produce reflex actions, this state of affairs does not last for long. Before many hours have passed the baby starts to learn, or to be more accurate its reflexes start to become more controlled.

As a result of this process its brain grows day by day—in effect, it develops new nerve fibres to deal with increasingly complicated behaviour. It learns how to use its eyes and ears more effectively to predict what is happening around it, and to vary the way it cries so that it receives the appropriate treatment, such as a change of clothing, a feed, a sleep, or being burped. Step by step over the next few years it will go on learning to control and develop its own reflexes. All the time it is learning self-control. By the age of five its brain will have reached half its final adult weight, and by the age of nine, almost ninety per cent of the final weight. So most of this self-control is learned in early life.

From whom does a baby learn these lessons? The most important influence is provided by the adults who have the main care of the baby, usually its parents. They affect the way the infant learns to control its own reflexes by the way they teach it to tolerate discomfort or pain, and to delay pleasure. They teach it to not-feel things. For example, a small child may be taught to wait for food until its mother is ready to feed it. It has to learn to not-feel hunger. Or it may be taught to say the magic word 'please' before it can take hold of a small gift. It learns to not-feel greedy. The parents carefully administer small doses of pain to teach all this self-control. (The word 'pain' is seldom used, since we prefer less evocative terms like 'frustration', 'discipline' or 'disappointment'.) Most of us were brought up the same way. We had to learn to wait for pleasurable experiences, and to tolerate the discomfort of not having our own way. As a result of millions of such lessons we learned to walk the correct way, and talk nicely, to use a potty by ourselves, to smile politely and say thank you, to use a knife and fork less clumsily, to read and write and draw properly or not at all, to be kind to little sister and not-feel angry at her, to let aunty kiss us and not-turn away, and all the other countless items of control and self-control which made us what we are today.

Each lesson enables the child to exert a little more control over its reflexes, so that it can do things for itself. The original reflexes were complicated enough, but as the learning proceeds the child's behaviour becomes infinitely more complex. Yet each action is the result of 'conditioned' or 'trained' reflexes. And each bit of conditioning requires control of feelings in order to be effective.

Schooled by pain

We can now return to the earlier question: suppose you have some kind of behaviour pattern which you know leads you into many minor breakdowns, and which you want to change. How do you achieve this? The answer should be simple. If you find yourself doing things you dislike doing, then don't do them! In practice it is far from easy. If you do a lot of notting, and looping then you will have tried many times to kick the habit, and you will have failed. Why are our most dangerous habits so hard to give up?

These habits which are hardest to give up are the ones which were learned the hardest way. They were learned not because of pleasant experience, but as a result of pain. Your worst habits are not only conditioned reflexes, but they are also those reflexes which were most thoroughly conditioned. More pain was used to teach you to behave this way than with all the other things you learned. Of course it is difficult to 'un-learn' habits which were taught this way! If learning the habit was painful in the first place, learning to be different will also be painful.

This point needs a little clarification. Learning to be different means you have to reverse the process by which you learned the bad habit in the first place. In other words, to learn a new way of doing something, first you have to unlearn the old way. You have to go back and start again. After all, you cannot stop being yourself, and suddenly turn into somebody else. Nor can you have a brain transplant. Change does not happen either just because the right person comes into your life and alters everything. Any change in your behaviour has to be accomplished by you alone, through learning to use what you already have in a different way. Unlearning anything is just as hard as learning it was in the first place. The things we learned easily are the easiest to change. And those we learned the hardest way are the hardest to change.

Mum and dad know best

If we take a closer look at how children are taught to behave then we can consider this question in more detail. Let's take the case of Graham, a man of above average intelligence who at 45 found that he was in a job he hated, married to somebody he did not like, and quite unable to face the thought of changing his life to please himself. Graham said he wanted to be able to stand up for himself better. Each time he tried, he failed. There were many things he could do, but he could not manage this. How had he learned to be the sort of person who tried to stand up for himself but failed?

His memories of childhood included the following sample of learning situations. When he was nine he got into the school football team, much to the pleasure of his father who had always fancied himself as a centre-forward. Father came to watch the match, shouted himself hoarse, and took over the boy's training. This consisted very largely of showing Graham that father's way of doing things was much better than Graham's. When Graham's keenness to go for yet another training session began to fade, his father looked very hurt and Graham put up with his own guilt feelings and dislike of football for his father's sake. After a time, Graham learned to admire his father's skill, instead of valuing and developing his own. Pleasing father was clearly more important than pleasing himself. He had learned how to not-play football, and how to not-upset his father. When Graham was 17 he fell in love with a girl his parents thought was beneath him. They went round to see the girl's parents, made a scene, forbade Graham to see her, phoned the school and insisted on closer supervision of their son. Graham today is quite unshakable in his conviction that all this had been for his own good, and that he was grateful for the way his parents handled the situation. His mother had been so upset she had nearly broken down, and she was overjoyed when Graham saved her all that worry. Graham had learned to be even more expert at not-upsetting his parents. At 19 Graham left school and took a job in a solicitor's office because he agreed with his parents that there was no future in being an art student, which Graham really preferred. He had a series of girl-friends but only took the nice ones home, eventually marrying the nicest of them, according to his mother.

Graham loved his parents and was convinced that they loved him. He said he had a happy, secure childhood—he could never remember his parents fighting. If they did so, it was never in front of him. His father taught him a great deal, how to play football, how to choose the right friends, how to respect older people and know your place. His mother taught him what kind of wife would be best for him. At 45 he still felt grateful, despite his mother's occasional accusation that he did not know the meaning of the word 'gratitude'. So where did it all go wrong?

The right way

What went wrong was that in so many of these learning situations Graham learned the 'right' way to run his life by being made to feel intolerably unhappy and then having to suppress his feelings. He had been taught to be second-rate, that he was not as good as his father, nor as sensitive and capable as his mother. He could never be better at anything than they were. Achievement to the growing Graham meant being nearly as good as his parents, but never quite making the grade. If he tried to stand up for himself and have his own special feelings they made a scene and he was forced to deal with their feelings rather than his own.

At some point in each of these lessons, Graham had felt very angry. He had felt furious with his father for shouting so much at the football match, for example, and for muscling in on his son's achievement in getting into the school team only to take over as if it had been his father's achievement. To learn how to be Graham, the boy had also learned to not-feel all this anger, to stand up for his parents, not for himself. Even today he was still doing this over the girl-friend incident, not standing up for how he felt, but feeling sorry for having caused so much trouble. And what would have happened in any case if Graham had showed even a fraction of his anger? Instead of being wrong in his choice of a girl to fall in love with, or for hiding their assignations from his parents, he would have been punished just for showing his anger.

So now Graham is stuck in a life he does not want, afraid to let everybody down, his boss, his wife, his children, his now elderly mother and father, and still unable to take the credit for having his own feelings. Above all he cannot please himself, or show when he is angry. The reasons for his failure to change are locked inside, held in place by the almost unimaginable rage of the small boy he once was, made to look ridiculous by his own parents, and taught to be second-rate just like them, with the added insult that he had to regard them as first-rate. All the things he now wants to change were learned the hard way—through unhappiness, not pleasure. That suppressed rage was the price Graham paid for being taught the right way to conduct his life. He is still paying that price, still holding his rage in check.

The general reasons why human beings learn so well is that they have a nervous system so developed that it can actually suppress pain, the pain of anger, rage, and the fear of what might happen if this rage ever got out. The way children are brought up uses this system. Children are taught to expect punishment for doing things their parents disapprove of. They are also taught self-control. That is to say, they learn to punish themselves if their parents are not around to do this for them and to not-feel the emotion their parents do not want them to feel.

Unlearning patterns of behaviour is made more difficult by the locked-in pain which was suppressed at the time the lesson was learned. This pain could not be felt at the time; it had to be not-felt. Not-feeling it pleased the child's parents. Clearly we need to look next at them.

6

The Parental Lie

We are mostly brought up to believe that of all institutions in our society the family is the cornerstone of the good life. We feel sorry for those who had no family. Families provide love and support, encouragement and discipline. An attack on the family is seen as an attack on all that is good in our version of civilization. At the head of the family stand the parents. Theirs is no easy task. But with selfless devotion they bring up their children through bad times as well as good times, giving them a helping hand through their little troubles, loving them come what may. We are taught that we should love, honour, and respect our parents. There is something sacred about parenthood.

But from time to time a subversive thought may creep surreptitiously between the cracks of our consciousness. When you were conceived were your parents dedicating themselves to a lifetime of selfless caring, or just having fun? Are all mothers thrilled to the core when presented with a baby? Do all fathers enjoy fatherhood? We have already seen that inside many of us is a part we would like to change but cannot, because of what our parents taught us—not through love, but through pain. The parts of ourselves which we can easily change may be flexible because they were taught through love. The difficult and most worrying parts of our personalities are a consequence not of parental love but something more like parental dislike, even parental hatred. Could it be that the most important of all social institutions, parenthood and family, is not what it seems? It is time to examine this thought and to inject a little reality into the propaganda which surrounds the family.

Family life

Of all your relationships the most formative is the one between yourself and the people who brought you up. For most people this means mother and father, but it could also be a nanny or series of nannies if your parents could afford them and wanted them, or grandparents, aunts, adoptive parents, and so on. You may have been amongst the youngest of many children, or in any case had a brother or sister ten or more years older than yourself. If so, he or she may have also had a major influence on how you were brought up. The term 'parent' will be used from now on to refer to any of the people carrying out a major parental role in your life, because this is easier than spelling out all the exceptions each time. Parents are the people who bring up children. The closer we look at their activities, the less sacred they seem.

Bringing up a child means teaching him how to behave in ways the parent approves by disciplining him whenever he exhibits behaviour of which the parent disapproves. Discipline is the use of pain to inhibit behaviour. You have your own unique set of loops, and your personal ways of notting because of the way your parents brought you up. When you have a breakdown of any sort—brief or lengthy —this is because you have been let down by what your parents taught you. Something they taught you to think of as true is in fact a lie.

To avoid breakdown you need to know which lies your parents taught you. You need to recognize and to feel once more the rage and the fear with which they hammered the lie inside you. You need to free the energy which became trapped inside your growing body by this process. It is no use waiting until you have a breakdown to do this. The rage must be dealt with harmlessly and safely if at all possible, not in the destructive burn-up of a breakdown.

It may be that you cannot feel anger towards your parents. If your parents were perfect, then this is understandable. But few parents are perfect. Nevertheless, if you feel nothing but love towards them, like Graham for example, it is hoped you will keep an open mind until you have read the whole argument. What you think of as 'love' may be the effect of parental propaganda. We can see this by looking at some more examples of the parental lie in action.

Lies in action

If you were to meet Malcolm, you would see a large, friendly and enthusiastic professional man. At 45 he is a very senior social worker, fast building himself a national reputation for his work on services for children. One day he confessed to his wife about an affair he had just finished after eight years. She began to have a breakdown, and as a result, Malcolm talked privately with the therapist. Some details of Malcolm's childhood emerged.

He was an only child of very loving parents. His father used to place Malcolm in the middle between husband and wife and embrace them both. 'I'm loving my darling wife through my darling son,' he would say. If Malcolm wanted anything for a birthday or Christmas present, it had to be the very best. Once he asked for an electric train, and was bought a massive layout which filled a large room and half the passage outside. He said he would like a microscope, and received equipment sophisticated enough for an advanced research scientist. The family would go away for day's outings in their car, and sit in it on seaside promenades, while the parents pointed at the passers-by, laughing, and congratulating themselves on not being as strange as other folk. Father boasted that he had married the most beautiful woman on earth, and that when Malcolm's turn came, he should choose only the best. Malcolm was left in no doubt that he was loved.

Faulty goods

At one point in the interview, he began to describe an incident to prove this. 'I'll show you how much they loved me,' he said. 'They even took me back.' Apparently, the young Malcolm had gone through a period of bad behaviour, being stubborn, rebelling against his parents, refusing food. His parents announced that they were not satisfied with him. They would take him back to the shop where they bought him, and exchange him for another little boy. However, if he changed his ways and became more loving and obedient, this would not be necessary. Malcolm said he could remember feeling puzzled. He had never seen the departments in stores where little boys were sold. So he refused to change. Both parents took him to the car, forced him inside and asked again. Again he refused to be a good boy in future. They drove to the corner of the road, and stopped. 'Look round,' they said. 'It may be the last time you see our house. Will you be good now, or do we take you back?' Still Malcolm refused. He can remember vividly to this day the place on the pavement where they eventually stopped the car outside a large department store in the nearby town. Till then he had not really believed that they would exchange him. But once more they asked, and opened the car door to drag him out and hand him back. He screamed and clung to the seat. They pulled. His resistance was broken at last. He begged to be allowed to stay with them, promising all they asked. Each promise was double-checked. 'And he would eat up all his dinner?' 'Yes', screamed Malcolm. 'And keep his room tidy?' 'Yes, yes.' At last the contract was agreed. He would be a proper, loving son, and they would take him back. He was six years old at the time.

This is a particularly dramatic example of a small boy being taught to obey his loving parents through the careful use of terror. What are we to believe? That Malcolm's parents really loved him? This is certainly what Malcolm believed. Why else would they keep him? All through his childhood the boy was given countless tokens of his parents' love. Was this real love? Or was it the propaganda with which any tyrannical regime perpetuates the lies upon which its tyranny is based? When Malcolm said his parents must have loved him because they 'took him back', he did not mean because they took him back to the shop, but because, despite all his failings, and giving the chance to obtain a better boy, his parents retained him. They were going to throw him out, but took him back into their lives. The words Malcolm used masked the terror he had felt, and echoed years of subsequent reminders that his parents loved him, despite the badness at his core. That love was a lie. You do not systematically torture a person you love, nor teach them they are evil inside.

Systematic torture

The systematic torture of Sylvia was much less dramatic, but only because there was no single, traumatic incident on which to focus what was done to her. Sylvia's mother grew up, the youngest child and only daughter of a Jewish tailor, in Poland. Before the holocaust she was shipped to Palestine. Six years later her parents, brothers, aunts and uncles were all dead. Sylvia was born just before the war ended, and from the beginning she knew she had to be the very best at everything. She enjoyed school, but her marks were never good enough, even if she was top in every subject, as once happened. In her spare time she had ballet lessons, music lessons, art classes, deportment, and a succession of language teachers. She excelled and excelled, but never enough for mother. Time after time her mother explained that she was only doing all this for Sylvia's sake, because she loved her. And it should be no effort to Sylvia: her uncle so-and-so was good at music, and another one at languages, and aunt such-and-such had been brilliant at dancing, so it was in Sylvia's blood, her mother said. She should be grateful for the opportunity. Not everyone had such a loving mother, who would work and slave at any menial task to pay for all those lessons in Sylvia's spare time. Sylvia was forced to agree.

Sylvia is still not sure why her mother could not have seen that one small girl could never replace a whole family; that success to excess would never right the wrong that had been done. She still lives with her mother, finds lovers she does not really like and lies about them to her parent. The nice Jewish boy her mother wants her to marry seems as far away as ever, and, should he turn up, just as dull to Sylvia. But Sylvia knows her mother loves her. The systematic torture of endlessly being brilliant, but never being good enough produced enough anger to burn the world. But the counter-propaganda from Sylvia's mother succeeded, and Sylvia could feel none of that anger. She had notted it out of existence. The lie on which Sylvia was brought up, that her mother really loved her, could remain undiscovered, and Sylvia too was forced to lie. As for the problem which had taken Sylvia to the therapist, surely there was a simple answer. It was just that she never kept friends. She made friends easily enough, but soon got bored with them, and had this strange feeling that they were not good enough for her. 'I am not sure I know how to love people,' she said.

Conditional love

Of course she was not sure: throughout her childhood

Sylvia had never experienced unconditional love. Her mother loved her only on condition that she excelled. If Sylvia dared to be less than perfect, then her mother showed anger, disappointment, disdain, not love. Now that Sylvia was grown up and needed to be able to give and to take love unconditionally, she did not know how.

Malcolm did not know how to love, either. His affair, and his marriage had been based on the idea of conditional love. He expected his wife to behave correctly, but deep in his heart he also knew that she could never really love him. Inside he was evil, just as his parents had said he was. His wife could only love him if he performed well, as a lover, as a breadwinner, as a father. When he and his wife made love, Malcolm was an expert performer, planning every move he made so that it looked passionate and spontaneous. His mistress was somebody he played like a violin. He used to call her his Stradivarius. He had taken up with the mistress because his wife had stopped showing any enjoyment in sex after she lost a baby. Malcolm had simply not known how to love her. He had been taught not about true love, but about power: how to lay down terms and conditions in a relationship and pretend this was love.

Malcolm and Sylvia are good examples to look at because each of them is a successful person by almost every standard you can think of. They are at the top of their professions. Their parents were devoted to them. They were not spoiled as children. They were encouraged and disciplined and given the best their families could provide. Neither of them regards life as a trial; most of the time they see it as a challenge they will always be able to face up to. Yet both Malcolm and Sylvia hide inside a successful life-style the seeds of major breakdown. They do not understand unconditional love.

Unconditional love

The point we have to face is this: can anything less than unconditional love truly be called love? If you love somebody then you value that person infinitely, with no terms and conditions attached. You do not count the cost of that love. To do so would belittle it. Obviously unconditional love is an ideal form of love. Love with strings attached is better than no love at all, you may think. But is it? If you can only be loved by another human being on condition that you modify your behaviour to suit his of her expectations then you are buying love. The price can be raised by the person you love, and all you can do about it is to pretend you do not mind. Your life is not owned by you, but merely rented. The person who says he loves you is really the landlord of your emotions, with power of eviction he can use anytime he wants. Such love is dangerous. If you know of no other way to love, then, like Malcolm and Sylvia, you can never have security in your own feelings. Some part of you has to be notted out of existence.

And these two people were among the lucky ones, according to all the propaganda about family and parenthood. What about all the people whose parents never even pretended to love them? Each one of us was at times neglected as a child, we exposed the raw nerve of the parental lie, pushing the patience of the parents to its limits in some way, so that one or other of them over-reacted. We saw our own parents break the rules they insisted we kept; we incurred their uncontrolled anger or provoked their worst fears, and were disciplined for doing so.

You may remember many such incidents, or you may be able to recall none. But assuredly they were there. Childhood in our society, perhaps in all societies, is a time when we are taught the terms and conditions under which we

54

can be loved. We are then taught to accept the propaganda that this is real love. When we are small and weak we have little alternative but to believe what we are told, to fall for the parental lie. But such love is not good enough for us when we become adults. It leaves us lonely and we have to hide our pain. We cannot for ever live out our lives meeting the expectations of our parents, following to the letter the small print in the contract, and believing we know about love.

7
The Parental Contract

The parental lie is built into the parental contract. Mothers and fathers very rarely love their children unconditionally. Usually they expect their child to behave in a certain way, and if he does not meet their expectations and misbehaves, they withdraw approval and will only love the child if their conditions are met. These conditions, taken together, form a kind of contract. If the child fulfils his side of the bargain he will be loved; if not he has broken the contract, and is punished. Maybe if children were exactly like their parents, and were born not only with their personalities complete, but also with nothing to learn for themselves, there would never be a conflict of expectations. But although children are similar to their parents, they are not the same. And demands are placed on them at school, and amongst their contemporaries, which their parents may never have encountered.

From time to time, therefore, every child is faced with a choice. Either he can please himself and break the contract, or please his parents and be unhappy. If he shows this unhappiness, he will probably be punished to enforce the contract. So the child learns to bottle up his feelings, to not-feel his unhappiness, or to lie about it, and to accept that there are times when he cannot win whatever he does. He may accept this fate silently, as Sylvia did, and Graham. Or he may accept it only after a major power-struggle with his parents, as Malcolm did. For some children, too, there are many power struggles, so that unsuccessful rebellion becomes a way of life. It is time to consider what happened to you. The way you personally bottle up feelings depends upon the terms and conditions written in the small print of the contract you had with your own parents. What were these?

What happened to you?

When faced with this question, people generally respond in one of three ways. Some of them know at once what the conditions were. They have been aware as long as they can remember that childhood was a long battle for truth and freedom, to succeed despite their parents. A second group find the question difficult because they say they cannot remember their childhood. Some of them say this is because it was so long ago, that their memory is hazy just because of this; others declare that childhood was a feature-less event, with nothing important happening so that they cannot be expected to remember it. A third group of people react strongly against the whole idea of criticizing their parents, and refuse to consider the question. They show immediately that the vital clause in the small print of their contract was that they had to love, honour, and obey their parents, even when angry with them, and let down by them. Loyalty mattered more than truth.

Whichever group you belong to there is a high probability that somewhere in your contract was at least one impossible clause. Because of this there is a part of you which you would like to change, but cannot easily do so. The best way to proceed, since everybody is different, is to give examples of some of the most commonly encountered impossible clauses. The effect of such a clause is that whatever the child does he cannot win.

Thou shalt not be sexual

Throughout western cultures, one of the most common of impossible clauses in the parental contract reads: 'thou shalt not be sexual'. Some parents enforce this through showing fear, others through showing anger. For example, a mother may seek to inhibit her daughter's adolescent sexual behaviour by showing fear—worrying about the girl staying out late, or about the company she keeps. Fear of sex on the part of the parents may be transmitted to boys and girls simply by displays of embarrassment at sexual questions, or by the subject never being mentioned. If anger is used, a common way this is done is to warn girls of the consequences of coming home pregnant; or to warn the boys that they will be severely punished if caught masturbating, or if they get somebody pregnant.

You may remember incidents from your own adolescence which indicate that you were expected not to be an independent sexual person, able to enjoy sex, pleased with your own body, and attractive to people for sexual reasons. Training to not-be sexual usually begins very much earlier than this, for it is in infancy that children are most frequently taught not to show off their sexual parts, or touch them, but to regard them as either dirty or unmentionable or both.

'Thou shalt not be sexual' is an impossible clause because sexuality—the way we express ourselves and fulfil our needs by being either a female or a male person—is the most important of all our human characteristics, not only emotionally and physically, but also intellectually and socially. Girls may be taught, for example, that it is unfeminine to be clever; boys that it is unmasculine to be beautiful. You almost certainly know intimately where it was that your own parents drew the line. If you overstepped this mark you were being sexual in an unacceptable way. You can probably remember at least one occasion on which you had either to please yourself and break the rules, or be unhappy and conform. How many people, for example, can honestly say that when they first discovered masturbation, and experienced their first orgasm, that they felt able to tell their own parents of the delight they felt? It is far more likely that you were either too scared to experiment 'down there', or felt too embarrassed by what you had discovered to be able to discuss the matter, let alone share your joy. Nevertheless, most people who discover masturbation despite their parents go on doing it. Yet if two people love one another unconditionally, guilt has no place in their relationship. Sex is not seen as dirty, or as something to be afraid of or angry about. Few parent-to-child relationships achieve this. It is no exaggeration to say that most parents teach their children to hide sexual feelings, or to lie about them.

'Don't exist'

The clause prohibiting or limiting sexuality belongs to a large group of impossible clauses, the 'don't exist' group. In effect the child is punished for showing some kind of ordinary behaviour which displeases the parent. An extreme example is contained in the maxim that children should be seen but not heard. A slightly less cruel, but related version applies to those who were often rebuked or more severely punished for speaking out of turn, daring to question parental authority, interrupting grown-up conversations, being a nuisance by demanding attention. Children need attention. They know they are important. To be treated with disdain or anger when they know they have something important to say teaches them to suppress feelings and to lie to their parents when there are matters they would prefer to share and discuss, but which they think will incur parental fear or anger.

Suppose, for example, that a child arrives home from school after being severely criticized by a teacher or bullied by other children. His attitude when he walks in shows how miserable he feels. This unhappiness could be put into proportion by kindness, understanding, by a chance to talk about it. Such help would enable him to express his anger and fear, to be comforted, to learn to discuss feelings, but also to know that it is permissible to have real, violent feelings when people are aggressive towards him. Let us imagine that his mother is exercising a 'don't exist' clause in their contract. She may simply take one look at the child, order him to be happy by telling him to 'cheer up', and carry on with her household chores. If he then shows anger, she will punish him for what he does, for making a noise, for example, or for throwing down his school books. Maybe she will hit him, or tell him sharply that he is always being bad-tempered, and that she and his father are increasingly impatient with this facet of his personality. Or she may just give him a long, nasty look. In effect he does not exist as a person unless he is careful all the time to behave in a way which suits his mother, because otherwise she will punish him, or ignore him and his real feelings. A child who grows up with this impossible clause in his contract is forced repeatedly throughout childhood to suppress his rage—not only rage at what is done to him outside the home, but also his rage at the lack of interest shown and the extra punishment he incurs for trying to get help inside the home. The child who is frequently told not-to-be a nuisance, not-to-be-noisy, not-to-be a show-off, not-to-do this and not-to-do that is being taught to not-be. He will develop advanced skills at not-existing: copying the crowd when he really wants to be different; never drawing attention honestly to his needs, particularly sexual ones; always afraid that if he showed his true self others would reject him. He will also grow up with very little tolerance of anything non-conformist, eccentric, or individually different. Instead of talking about his feelings he will disguise important aspects of them, or bottle them up, notting them and himself out of existence. Perhaps you are like this.

'Don't succeed'

An equally common group of impossible clauses in the parental contract centres around the control of every child's natural need for achievement. In effect these clauses tell the child he will not be loved if he succeeds. We saw one example of this earlier in the case of Sylvia, the replacement child. Any child who is a second-best replacement is likely to have this clause in his or her contract. A woman may have a still-birth, or lose a boy-child, and then give birth to a girl-child, or vice-versa. The surviving child grows up never quite good enough. Its achievements never receive the success they warrant. If, for whatever reason, you were expected always to be perfect as a child, then you were being asked to perform the impossible. And today you are just as likely to punish yourself for what you see as 'failures', but which other people would give their eye-teeth to have achieved. You bottle up this lack of permission to receive praise; you need more than the average, but can never bring yourself to ask for it.

'Don't succeed' can also mean 'don't be different'. Children from large families often have different needs which their mother cannot recognize, and she therefore tries to treat the children the same, even when this causes severe distress to one of them. For example, she may give exactly the same rights to the youngest as to the oldest. Or she may intervene in quarrels and insist that toys are shared equally, even when one child has the greater need for the toy. An example of this would be a squabble over paints, arising because one child is the more talented artist, while the other is jealous.

Some children are taught that they are only truly loved if they are ill. Gerald's mother, for example, was a writer of children's books, and never had time for her son unless he was ill and she felt guilty enough to stop work. Today Gerald is nearly 40, lives with his mother, and spends about a third of each year away from work either having attacks of nervous depression, or being treated for what he, almost proudly, calls 'obsessional neurosis'. She is solicitous when he produces symptoms of disturbed behaviour, but only if they are extreme enough to merit treatment from a real doctor. At all other times she ignores him. He is unmarried, lonely, and very shy. He is also afraid of succeeding in his work and in his social life. Meanwhile her books are selling very well, painting an ideal picture of childhood.

Some parents show massive intolerance of failure. This may be intended to teach the child how to succeed, but in reality it teaches him how to fail. 'Don't talk to me about your failures, I'm only interested in success' sets up an impossible conflict in the child. Children, like every other kind of people, need to fail in order to learn. A child inevitably fails at many things. Not to be able to share this experience with someone who cares limits the usefulness of failure. But such a child soon discovers that a really spectacular failure will gain far more attention from the parent than a small success. So the child learns how to be a better failure, and may even make a career of it, and become a permanent rebel against its parents' standards.

'Be grateful'

One of the most insidious of impossible clauses in parental contracts is the clause which demands gratitude. The child is taught that he or she can only be truly loved by showing heart-felt gratitude for all that the parent has done for him. Perhaps one parent makes it clear that mother and father only stayed together for the sake of the children, and they should therefore be grateful. Or the slightest extra bit of care and attention has to be received with gratitude to avoid a long speech on the 'look at all I've done for you' theme. Some parents stress that their children are much better off than were the parents at their age: when they were kids they were made to work; beaten up regularly; never given enough to eat; had very cheap birthday presents; would never have dared to answer back like that; were in the army or the factory; and made endless sacrifices without recognition. But children are greedy, self-centred, rude, noisy, impolite these days, and not at all like the little angels they used to be, at the time of their parents' childhood.

The problem with having to supply gratitude on demand is that it is a feeling which only the truly enslaved can accurately counterfeit. To feel grateful you have to have been done a favour of large proportions. To be grateful for everything is impossible, because not everything you are supposed to feel grateful for is equally worth having. Some people brought up this way spend much of their time pretending that favours they did not even want were like manna from heaven. When a child is brought up on this clause he is being taught the surest way there is to lie about his own feelings.

Parental tyranny

Any regime which demands the impossible from its citizens and then enforces its authority against even the slightest rebellion is tyrannical. It is also dependent upon its propaganda apparatus. The family is no exception. Children who are taught to not-exist learn to accept the label of 'shy' or 'quiet', and the parents who use this label have, as a result, an effective piece of propaganda with which to place the blame for their child's failures on the child, rather than accepting their own responsibility. Children who are given the label of 'bad-tempered' or 'moody' begin to live up to their titles. At least this way they know who they are. They come to believe that their parent loves them in spite of the label, despite the 'innate' or 'instinctive' tendencies they have been *taught* to have.

And the propaganda takes over. It becomes enshrined in the child's image of himself, an image around which his adult life is henceforth built. So there are people who see themselves as asexual, are ashamed of being sexual, or think themselves less than normally sexual; as extremely patient despite a stormy childhood full of power struggles, because they eventually mastered their 'bad temper' by being bullied into not-feeling anger; as naturally inclined to fail, because their parents always said they were not very good at anything much, and the parent had to be right. When they need to change this view of themselves, they are faced with a very difficult task.

Parents are not always right. Being a parent is hard enough without the necessity to be perfect. Perhaps they do their best. But it is part of the propaganda to accept without further question that when their best is not good enough this somehow excuses them. Above all we need to question their worst failures; the ones which resulted in our own major difficulties, the parts of ourselves which are hardest to change.

8

Better Parenting

The part of you that has been there longest is the child you once were. This child is still inside you; the rest has grown around it. When you need to change and cannot, the child-like part of you wants to grow up but is too angry or afraid to do so. It feels again the intolerable unhappiness with which it was once trained by your parents. So it lies. It tells the untruths it was taught to tell. How can you enable it to grow and face the truths of your life; the parts you know you want to change if only you could face up to them? The only way is through better parenting, being a better parent to yourself than your real parents were to you so long ago.

It may help you to see this task in a wider, historical perspective. For centuries people have fought for the right to be free. They have demanded an end to oppression, struggled for liberty, equality, and fraternity, and a chance to choose their own way of pursuing happiness. Our version of civilization looks back on a proud history of success as adults have shaken off the yoke of tyranny. But the fight goes on, as, for example, women and minority racial groups demand that discrimination against them on the grounds of sex and colour must end. Most of this revolutionary fervour throughout the ages has been and still is on behalf of the adult. In the privacy of their own homes, a married adult couple have the inalienable right to oppress their children. Only when that child grows up can he set himself free.

Know your rights

The collective human experience of our culture is that to end any species of tyranny people have to insist upon their rights. To be a better parent to yourself, you have to know your rights, and to exercise them. Each impossible clause in a parental contract is a denial of rights. The 'good parent' is above all somebody who acknowledges the rights of the child. What are these?

You have the right to have, and to express your own feelings. If you were taught not to speak until spoken to, you were being denied the right to your own feelings. Today you have the right to speak even when not spoken to—and you may acknowledge this, grant it to others, and exercise it for yourself whensoever and howsoever you please. You have the right to show how you truly feel. You are the only person in the world who can feel your own feelings. Those feelings are unique and important. You will waste and damage them if they are not used, and the world will be worse off as a result, because it will finish up with a second-best you, not the best you it could otherwise have. If you were taught to go away and not be a nuisance, then exercising your right to have and express your own feelings means staying, and being a nuisance when necessary. If you were taught never to show off, remember you have the right to be pleased with your successes, to let others know you are pleased, to collect the acclaim that is due, and to recognize that this deprivation in childhood no longer need rule your adult life. You have the right to feel and express your sexual feelings honestly, and the right to have these respected and understood by other people. They do not have the right to impose their view of what you ought to feel on you; nor do you have this right over them.

66

You have the right to love and to be loved without terms and conditions. If there is any small print in your love contracts, or if you are placing any hidden clauses in the contracts you offer to other people then this right is being denied. You will be safest and healthiest if there is at least one person in the world with whom you have a relationship based on unconditional love. Of course, you cannot exercise this right through force; nor can others force you to love them unconditionally. Unconditional love means you will be vulnerable. You have that right, too.

You have the right to change, and to grow, and to fail. Your parent may have taught you never to appear inconsistent, but today you have that right. He or she may have taught you to stay childish in many things, never to grow, or not to grow until you reached a certain standard. For example, you may have been told repeatedly to wait until you were old enough, to wait till you were their age, to do the right thing at the right time, to not-exist until certain terms and conditions were fully met. Now you have the right to grow at your own pace. You can change if you wish. You do not have to wait until the time is ripe. It never, in any case, ripens on schedule for all the important events of life—falling in love, conceiving and giving birth, having original ideas, losing loved ones, dying. Now you can act in unripe time.

And you can fail. You do not have to be perfect, not for yourself nor for anybody. And you can succeed. You do not have to please anyone else by failing in any way. Changing, growing, and failing are all ways you can now behave because these were always your right. Today you have the freedom to exercise them.

You have the right to be alone. Perhaps the impossible clauses in your contract were to do with always knowing

67

your parents would be there to help you. To break this clause is to exercise a fundamental right to be a person as fully as this is possible. You cannot for ever have some-body on whom to lean and still exercise your fundamental right to be human. You are your own best protection. You have the right to reject as a lie any impression your parents gave you to the contrary.

You have the right to please yourself, and the right to exercise this right any way you choose. You are unlikely to grant that right to those who please themselves at cost to you; and if you are free of contamination from parental tyranny, then it is equally unlikely that you will please yourself through harming others and giving them fewer rights than you demand for yourself. If you know you are doing this, you would be wise to consider how you were taught to do it, and how it felt when you were being trained.

You have the right to be the first in a long line of successful human beings, and the right to be the last in a long line of scared and angry failures. You may feel that it is disrespect-ful, or disloyal to be a better parent than were your own parents. They may be people who would have been angry with you for thinking yourself capable of doing better. The thought that you might succeed where they failed might have frightened them. If so, this is why you will probably feel disloyal. But any such feeling is only caused by the long reach of their fear and anger at their own failure. You can put an end to that ancestral ghost.

Your own good parent

To be your own good parent you have to know and to exercise your rights; but a good parent does more than simply accede rights to its child. It nurtures, fosters, encourages. Perhaps your parent taught you to neglect yourself, to deny yourself the full value of your body, personality, skills, opportunities, and friendships. Perhaps you discourage yourself. Why do you do this? You do it because you are still trying to please your own parent. Just as part of you is still the child you once were, so another part of you consists of a built-in parent. When, in childhood, your reflexes were being trained, you learned to behave the way your parents wanted you to, even when they were not present. Today when you cannot do what you really want to do, and find that this is an insurmountable problem, this is because you would rather discourage yourself than face up to the anger and the fear of the built-in parent.

To be truly honest about your own feelings means ending the influence of the parental lie. To do this you have to flout the authority of the parent. There is a rule somewhere which they taught you to respect, but which you have to break. In order to break this rule and set yourself free, you may have to go through a painful unlearning process. There are three stages to this process.

How to unlearn

First, it may be necessary to feel once more the terrible anger of the thwarted child. This is the anger which your parents taught you to suppress. It is quite unlike the anger of most adults; there is nothing calm or calculated about it, nothing forgiving or gentle. It is a limitless, total, destructive rage. It is the fury with which a young child can turn, full of hatred, to its parents, and say with total sincerity that he hates them, that he would like to kill them, that they have never loved him, that he wishes they were dead. Such rage demands the utter destruction of the parent. To civilized sensibilities it is shocking, and frightening. Those who work with the victims of long-term breakdown know it well. Psychologists who work in

69

therapy groups to promote better growth in the lives of people who have medium and short-term breakdown also recognize it. In a more sinister way, perhaps, those who harness it for military purposes probably know it best of all. When you have a breakdown this is what seems ready to get out.

Within the child who has been denied his rights and placed over and over again into the position of having to do the impossible, this rage gathers and remains and is hidden. Usually it is also protected by fear; the fear of what would happen should this annihilating force escape. It may be the fear of being alone if the parent was destroyed by the child's rage; it may be the fear of retribution; it may be the fear that the child too would be annihilated, by its own anger. A layer of anger is covered by a layer of fear, and this in turn is covered by another layer of anger. Inside many people who have breakdowns is a layer-cake of anger and fear, a time-bomb of notted destructive power, which, at the acute phase of the attack, explodes.

It may not be possible for you to put an end finally to the parental authority which still holds you to the parental lie. If you can do so, this will only come about by your being honest about the feelings you suppressed in childhood. You are entitled to feel angry at what they have done to you, and yet for most of us, this anger is difficult to express. The problem is to take the risk of feeling anger as the child knows it, and not as the adult allows it. Letting go of all your inhibitions, risking the full destructive power of that anger, is not easy. It demands a complete loss of self-control and a safe place where you can scream and shout, kick, punch, scratch, and smash. A well-run therapy group can be safe. Your own private bedroom, with pillows to punch, can also serve. Many people benefit from doing this. Most report that their main difficulty lies in feeling ridiculous at first. This is understandable, because to let out the total rage of the child within, you have to become a child once more. Not surprisingly, when you do this, you feel childish. But it is worth mentioning the alternative. If you have such rage inside you, and most people who have been 'brought up' have it, then the only other way you will ever let that rage out is by having a breakdown of some kind. Losing your temper in a 'real-life' situation and having the tantrum which you need is far more dangerous than having the tantrum on your own terms in a safe place.

Excuses, excuses

The first stage in the unlearning process is to feel the anger. The second stage is to stop making excuses for the parent who caused it. There is no excuse. Many people find this hard to learn. They argue that mother and father did their best. Times were hard, perhaps, or their parents had a hard life when they were young. One of the commonest excuses of all is that the parents did not know any better because of how they were brought up. These may be reasons. But there is no excuse. Consider the traditional defence of the war criminal, that he was only taking orders from higher authority and carrying them out. This may explain why he acted as he did, but it is no excuse. If your parents denied you your rights as a human being in any measure at all in response to 'orders' from higher authority —whether this was their parents, or their contemporaries —then their defence is no better than that of the war criminal. You will not be able to connect your present feelings with your buried anger if you fail to face squarely the fact that they did not even for one moment have to treat you as a non-person. It was their choice. If you wish to be free from the threat of nervous breakdown, you must make a different choice from the one they made. If you make excuses for your parents, you are merely reserving the right to make excuses for yourself.

And that is the third stage, to stop making excuses for yourself. It is right to feel angry. It is fair to place the blame where it belongs. But once you have done this, you must take full responsibility for yourself. Henceforth, never treat yourself as a non-person. To become a better parent to yourself, and to succeed in those respects where they failed, you have to grasp firmly the responsibilities they shirked. This is no easier to do than the other two stages were. But if you simply feel all the anger, blame it on your parents, and stop at that, then you have made no progress. Ahead of you lies only an empty future—the loneliness of the long-distance tantrum. Perhaps you know people who seem to be permanently embittered by what their parents did to them. They are dedicated to negative living. Better not join them.

Love yourself unconditionally

It is often said that you cannot love others unless you first learn how to love yourself. As long as you continue to work within the limitations of a parental contract based on conditional love, you will have a compelling reason to love other people either less than you love yourself, or more than you love yourself. If you love them less, then it will be easiest for you to take power over them, to demand that they love you out of duty and respect for your innate superiority. Many men appear to take this view of their wives and children. Women and children are seen by them as lesser beings, not fully capable of finer feelings, without the same glorious strength of the adult male. Such people dare not be weak—a weak man is contemptible in his quasi-femininity. But if you love yourself more than you love others, and your strength is demolished by a failure at work, by marital failure, or by ill-health, the conditions upon which you demand love will not be met and you will be alone and lonely. Such men crumble rapidly under their breakdowns. And if you love others more than you love yourself, you are no safer. You place all the power in their hands. You spend your life helping them, but getting no help for yourself when you need it. The doormat is your model. Worry will be your burden.

If you are your own best parent, succeeding where your real parents failed, you can love yourself unconditionally. You can exercise your rights as a fully-paid-up member of the human race. You have a firm base of confidence from which to love others unconditionally. When others fail to encourage you, you can encourage yourself. All you do with your life is your own responsibility. If you feel anger or fear it will be all yours, not part yours and part your parent's. You will own your life full and clear, not be the tenant on behalf of somebody who never really knew you.

9
Step by Step

To have complete immunity from breakdown, you need to be able to be totally honest with yourself all the time, and to have taken full responsibility for your life by unloading finally all the hidden anger, resentment, fear, and anxiety which accumulate during childhood. This is an ideal solution, but it is not one which the vast majority of us accomplish overnight. Very few people are able to wake up one morning and issue a communiqué to the world that they have triumphed for ever over anger, fear, and depression. The once-and-for-all solutions to unhappiness exist only in fairy tales. The best way to obtain the miracle of freedom is the most practical—to get there step by step. Where, in practical terms, should you start?

Relieving the pressure

There are several practical steps you can take to relieve pressure on yourself. We have already seen that breakdowns result from a build-up of intolerable unhappiness inside a person. When you next have a short-term breakdown, it will be for two reasons. First, there will be an immediate set of circumstances which act as the 'last straw'. This will take the form of a problem which gets out of proportion—a problem at work, say, or a financial worry, or, more likely, an incident which arises at home and produces a conflict between yourself and somebody close to you, such as a spouse, child, or lover. The problem acts as a trigger, and the breakdown occurs so that either you lose your temper, or you find yourself intolerably miserable and unable to stop weeping. You will probably

74

be over the breakdown in a matter of minutes or hours. But the immediate set of circumstances which acted as the trigger is only part of the cause. The second part is the unhappiness you already had inside you before the trigger was pressed. You can start to relieve pressure on yourself right now by beginning to reduce your internal fund of unhappiness.

First, you need to understand this unhappiness. It is a direct result of the way you treat yourself. In effect it is a self-imposed punishment. When you were a child your parent punished you for failing to live up to his or her expectations. Today when you fail to do the impossible, you punish yourself, because you have taken over from your parent. Secondly, if you know that you are punishing yourself, you can see that this is something you no longer have to do. You are in charge of your life now, not your parent. You can do a better job than your parent did. The world will not come to an end if you give up punishing yourself on behalf of your parent. Thirdly, you need to be able to recognize the ways in which you punish yourself. The most common ways are being aggressive with yourself, withdrawal from others, guilty feelings, shame, embarrassment, jealousy and possessiveness, and feelings of inferiority. Let us look at each of these in turn. They are unlikely to apply to you personally in equal measure, but as you read through them, remember that if the cap fits, you can wear it. Try to see what it is you do personally. If you feel sure that you do not do any of the things mentioned, then think carefully about them, and see if you know somebody else who does.

Attacking yourself

Being aggressive with yourself is a common way of reacting to pressure. What happens is that you attack yourself for having failed to achieve a target you have set yourself. Or

75

at least, that is what appears to happen. In fact, what you do is to attack yourself the same way your parent would have attacked you.

Suppose, for example, that you have been feeling for some time that you have too much to do, that everybody is expecting far too much of you, that there are not enough hours in the day to do it all, and that if you get asked to do one more thing this will be the last straw. It is a common enough feeling, one that most people will recognize. It can happen at work, or in the home, or because your relatives or friends are apparently expecting more of you than usual. Under such circumstances, as the targets pile up which you are expected to meet, you find that you have forgotten something. Perhaps you fail to turn up for an appointment, forget to telephone somebody, find you have forgotten an anniversary or birthday, or forget to post an important letter. When this happens you find that you punish yourself by becoming much more aggressive internally. Some people physically attack themselves, by hitting themselves on the head, slapping their own thigh, punching their arm or hand, or by hitting a hand or their head against a wall. They feel the need to hurt themselves, and they nearly always do this using the same system or one very similar to the method their parent would have used. Thus leg slappers were once children whose legs were slapped; head hitters were once children whose ears were boxed, and so on.

Insulting yourself

Self-directed aggression is often verbal, too. What you do is to give yourself a severe ticking-off; you grumble at yourself and tell yourself to stop being a fool, to grow up, to get properly organized, or to pull yourself together. Or you may call yourself names, just as your parent may have said you were a fool, or clumsy, or an idiot, or not safe

76

to be let out, or a good-for-nothing layabout who can not be trusted with any simple task. You may find that you do this in your own head, or out loud, or that you do it in conversation with the person you have let down. For example, people who miss appointments or forget anniversaries often begin their apologies by going into a bout of self-directed aggression; saying they are sorry, and that you must think they are totally unreliable, or a complete idiot, and so on. There is also a more complicated long-term reaction caused by self-directed aggression—self-injury through illness. Some people appear to punish themselves by having headaches, by letting migraine take over, or by suffering a recurrence of back pain or breathing problems. Others become constipated. At its extreme, when there has been a long history of previously unsolved short-term breakdown, self-directed aggression can take the form of major self-destructive acts, such as wrist-slashing, over-dosing, or similar suicidal reactions. But these are extreme responses, and while they illustrate the same principle—that the person concerned is punishing himself in accordance with what he feels the parent really wants him to feel—they are outside our present scope. Far more commonly, self-directed aggression is either a physical or verbal attack on yourself, or you may break something which belongs to you and which you value.

Great expectations

All these ways of reacting to pressure appear at the time to be a response to what other people seem to expect of you. You have tried to do too much because others expected this of you. But did they? If you think back to the last time this sort of thing happened then the truth will probably emerge that you were really expecting too much of yourself. You put yourself under pressure. You were trying too hard to be the sort of person you were taught to try to be—an impossible person, one who could do everything perfectly, one who could please everybody or be everywhere at once. In your case, do you remember that most of the extra things you promised to do were because *you* offered to do them? Why did you offer? The chances are that you offered because people would otherwise get the impression that you were not perfect! So, when events proved that you were not perfect after all, you punished yourself. Why do you punish yourself for not being perfect? You do not have to please that parent of yours any longer. Your parent was asking the impossible. But you know better than to do this.

You can immediately relieve some of the internal pressure on yourself by giving up trying to be perfect. The built-in parent who wants you to be perfect is wasting his time. He can go away and play somewhere else.

Banishing yourself

Many people punish themselves through withdrawal. They deprive themselves of something they really want by a self-imposed sentence of banishment or imprisonment. Suppose, for example, that you are asked by a group of friends to go out for a drink or a meal. You really want to go with them. But you make some excuse, you have to stay in to wash your hair, or to get the next part of a job done, or perhaps to get round to a task which you have been putting off for weeks. What you actually do is to punish yourself by feeling alone, lonely, and miserable. You have convinced yourself that you do not belong in the company of happy people. You may say that 'for your sins' you have to stay at home, and not enjoy yourself. For what sins? Why is it that from time to time you banish yourself into outer darkness?

One common reason which may apply to you is that children are often presented with the impossible task of having to be happy all the time. If they are seen to look miserable, they are ordered to be happy by being told to get on with something, or to cheer up, or to stop making other people miserable. Usually the reason why they feel unhappy is that something has either frightened or angered them which they cannot understand or put into words. Because the parent does not want to know what caused the unhappiness, and will not spare the time to find out, the child is banished until it cheers up. In time it learns to do this without being ordered. When you banish yourself, you may be making the assumption that unless you are happy, other people will not want to know you. This would have pleased your parent, but your parent is no longer in charge of your life. So why not take the risk of checking out your friends to see if they prefer your absence to your unhappiness? Punishing yourself for not knowing why you feel miserable is a sure way of staying even more miserable. If your friends are worth having then they will certainly not wish that on you. They would far prefer you to be able to talk about what is bothering you, so that you can find out what it is, and help you feel better about things. If you want your parent to triumph, and to have the power to make you banish yourself when you feel unhappy, then carry on and do so. But if you would rather reduce your fund of internal unhappiness, then next time you feel this way, tell your parent to get banished, and stay in the land of the living yourself.

Many ordinary parents, doing their best to bring up their children in a far from perfect world, teach them to feel guilty, ashamed, and embarrassed. The things you feel guilty, ashamed, or embarrassed about are probably the ones you know your parent would not want you to enjoy. You might like to put the book down for half an hour or so and make a list of them. People vary tremendously in the triggers for these feelings. When you find yourself doing things you know you are not supposed to enjoy, or which you should not find amusing or pleasurable, then you punish yourself with bad feelings.

How to enjoy yourself

Now you are in charge of your own life, you can diminish your inner store of bad feelings by getting rid of some of the items you are supposed to not-enjoy. It is time to take off some of the restraints your parent imposed, and which you have perpetuated. Over the next few days find, or better still make, time to enjoy at least one thing your parents would have disapproved of. And make sure also that somebody else is told that you have done this and enjoyed it. Without apologizing! Of course, everybody's list will be different, and the suggestions which are made in books do not fit everybody's circumstances. Nevertheless, here are a few.

If your parent was always moaning about money, go and do something extravagant. Buy yourself something you cannot afford, and then face up to your own feelings of guilt. They are coming from your built-in parent, and they stem from the impossible demand that you should not enjoy yourself without the parent's permission. Each time you feel yourself worrying, or feeling guilty, tell the parent in your head to grumble at somebody else. You have the right to act without permission, and to spend too much money, and you have taken over that right and exercised it. It is not your parent's business when you enjoy yourself, and that is the end of the matter.

If you are embarrassed by 'dirty' jokes, find a bookshop where there are magazines or books which contain this kind of joke or cartoon. Buy a copy of a publication containing one which makes you blush, and learn the joke by heart. Then find somebody you can tell it to. If you get the joke wrong, or find that at the last minute you cannot go through with the challenge, do not give up. This is what the tyrannical side of your parent wants you to do, but you are now learning to run your own life. Tell the parent in your head to do something rude, and start the joke again. If it falls flat, no matter. The important part of the exercise is to 'desensitize' or unlearn one of your inner fears, so that something in future will be less embarrassing. This is done by sending the parent packing. Whether or not you get a laugh from the joke is immaterial.

Another suggestion you might like to follow, and which has helped many people to defuse their hidden anger and fear, is to give yourself permission to be noisy during sex. This exercise works for many reasons. It acts as an antidote to hidden anger at having to be quiet as a child, to stop yourself showing off in front of embarrassed adults, to worrying about what the neighbours think, to not being fully sexual, to letting go when you feel good, and many more. Above all it sets you on the road to the sheer enjoyment of being yourself.

The sexual act, of course, can be with a partner or by yourself. All over the world in recent years, psychologists working in the women's movement and in therapy groups have found that when people learn to be uninhibited in the privacy of their own homes, and to make a noise while masturbating, that they are also forced to face up to parental controls left over from childhood. Maybe you know this already, and never let an opportunity pass without vocalizing in full voice! But it is surprising how many of us do not. We perform sexually, instead of enjoying ourselves. This pleases the parent in the head, who was never quite sure that it was a 'good thing' to let yourself be sexual. It is.

Coping with jealousy

Jealousy and possessiveness are among the most difficult

of all feelings to deal with. Time after time they trigger off breakdowns in people's lives, connecting together the unhappiness of a present situation with the deeply hidden reservoir of childhood unhappiness. The root cause of the jealousy reaction is fear—fear of being left alone, of being deserted by an angry, careless, or cruel parent. But jealousy also uses anger, the childlike rage we feel when something we want to cling to, to own for ourselves is forcibly taken away from us. We would rather destroy it than not have it. A person who is being hurt by jealousy often swings violently between fear and anger. He punishes himself for fear by being angry, and for anger by feeling afraid.

We can see this more clearly if we consider an example, in this case an instance of mild jealousy. More extreme jealousy works just the same way. Suppose a married couple go to a party, and enter a crowded room where people are standing drink-in-hand and chatting. The couple begin together, but then get talking to different people, and find they are separated. We will imagine this on video tape, and stop the action just at the point where she looks round, finds he is missing, and sees him chatting to a beautiful woman in a low-cut dress.

Suppose we call the husband George, and the wife Mary. Mary probably does not realize straight away that she feels jealous. She experiences a sense of being separated from George, and this connects with her childhood fear of being abandoned by her parent. If she has been more afraid than usual of being left by George lately, this will be a strong feeling. Also, if she was often abandoned by her parent it will be a strong feeling. Otherwise she may not feel fear. Secondly, she may feel anger. George is talking to somebody who looks sexually attractive on the surface, but whom she does not know. For the moment at least, he seems to prefer this person to her. So she is being rejected. He is also having more fun than she is.

She is placed in a position of having to compete with a complete stranger, for control of something which is hers by right. Feelings like these will take place inside Mary if her parent used to force her to fight for whatever fun she had out of life, and if the parent used to act arbitrarily to stop her fun by, for example, taking away toys, or putting a stop to friendships or activities he did not approve of. In other words, Mary's jealous reaction will depend on whether or not it connects up with parental punishment for showing fear at being abandoned, or for anger at having something taken away from her.

Asking for trouble

Mary now acts on her jealous feelings. She pushes her way through to George, and introduces herself as his wife. Then she says that there is an old man-friend in the opposite corner who she knows will want to talk to George, and she steers him away. She makes George angry, getting him to punish her because she has been silly to think he would desert her; and she punishes herself for feeling angry by wasting her time looking for the old friend who is the most boring person present.

Feelings of jealousy and possessiveness always force us to punish ourselves. We nearly always end up hurting other people so they will hurt us. The only winner is the parent in the head, who expects the impossible of you; that you can actually own somebody else's life and feelings. Now you are in charge of your own life you can tell the parent that nobody owns you, least of all the parent. There is no longer any need to have a parent or a parent-substitute around to give meaning to your life. You do not belong to anybody but yourself. Nobody is your property.

You are invaluable

Nor do you need to punish yourself by feeling inferior.

The reservoir inside you may consist of many feelings that you were taught to have which reduce you in your own eyes. As you set about step by step freeing yourself from the impossible demands of your parent, it may help you to remember that you are changing and growing all the time. You do not have a fixed value. Things which you may think you always do badly are things you can get better at. You can learn all your life. You will never be too old to change.

Ultimately, feeling inferior is connected with the impossible demand from your parent of never having been born. Parents often wish, for many reasons, that their children had not been conceived, or had never been born. This is understandable. But it is not a good excuse for you to punish yourself. Your life is there. You are living it. It is your very own. Life itself is invaluable, and so are you.

10
Other People

People rarely have breakdowns alone and unaided, although they often find themselves in this situation during the acute stage. What part do other people play in helping you preserve your tendency to have breakdowns? How do they help you to build up unhappiness? The question is an important one. Before we answer it, let us consider why it is so important.

One reason is that the pattern of breakdown invariably involves other people. It begins with a problem, and since so much of life is shared with others through relationships with lovers, spouses, children, relatives, and colleagues, many of the problems which we face are about how to get on with these people. The second stage of a breakdown comes about because we cannot communicate with other people. So they are involved here, also. When our relationships with them break down, we begin to experience a breakdown in internal communication—the relationship with ourselves. During the third stage, and while the acute stage is upon us, we are cut off from other people. But to make a full recovery, we need to restore communication, first with ourselves, and then with the people around us. We have to learn to trust ourselves again, and to re-establish our trust in others. The recovery stages are only going to be complete if we can make better and safer relationships, not only with people we knew before the acute stage of the breakdown, but also with people we did not know before.

We have already seen that it is possible to make many generalizations about breakdowns, and about the people who are most susceptible to them. For example, all break-down victims experience a loss of self-control, and have to put themselves in the care of others. Every breakdown crisis is centrally concerned with a feeling that life has no value and no meaning. Breakdown victims tend to be active at notting and looping. It can also be said that the people who go through the worst of long-term crisis often have a chronic difficulty in making and maintaining healthy relationships. Part of your own susceptibility to short and long-term breakdown lies in the nature of your existing relationships. Obviously it will help you to learn how to look at them more clearly.

Looking at relationships

So let us assume that you are adopting a step-by-step approach, and weeding out all the tendencies you have which will lead you into short, medium, or long-term breakdown. You have already decided to be honest with yourself about your own feelings. You know what your rights are, and you wish to exercise them. You are learning to change, and particularly to take over from your parent so that you are in charge of your own life. You have started to give yourself permission to destroy the fund of unhappiness left over from childhood by telling the parent in your head to leave you alone. In practical terms you are on your way. The only obstacle you are likely to meet consists of the other people with whom you share your life.

And this can seem a major obstacle. Suppose, for example, that you recognize a tendency in yourself to be dishonest, or less than fully honest, about your sexual feelings. It is one thing to be more honest with yourelf, to admit that you want more than you get, or that you are not enjoying sex. It is quite another task to tell your partner, or, if you do not have a regular partner, to find somebody you can tell this to. Many people have marriages which were fine sexually when they began. Over the years feelings have been hidden to avoid hurting somebody you love. Your dishonesty has been encouraged by all sorts of messages from your partner, messages which show that if you say how you truly feel you will anger, hurt, or otherwise upset somebody you depend on and are close to. You may, like thousands of others, be faced with a conflict. On the one hand, you know you are unhappy, and that this can lead to breakdown unless you are able to be more honest about sex. But on the other hand, if you try to be honest, you end up hurting somebody, and produce a conflict with that person. It looks as though you cannot win.

Or suppose you are a parent, and find yourself increasingly at odds with one of your children. You worry about the child, about its attitude to life and to other people, about the child's work at school, about scrapes it gets into or company it keeps, or maybe about acts of delinquency such as stealing or violence. You wonder where you went wrong, and where it will all lead. Communication between you and this young person has become very difficult, so that sometimes it breaks down altogether. Being honest with yourself about the fear and anger you feel is a first step. But how can you communicate this to the child? The relationship seems so firmly established. Somehow the child never seems to give you the chance to change it. You begin to feel that it is too late to change, and that whatever you do will be wrong.

The new you

Perhaps you are unmarried, and have no children. Relationships at work or with your neighbours and friends may currently be the most important focus in your life. These people are used to seeing the 'old' you, the person you have been all the years you have known them. When you begin to weed out your tendencies to have small break-downs, and to get rid of the unhappiness inside you, this starts a whole set of changes in your life. If you have never spoken openly about how you feel, or about your parents, and suddenly start coming out with momentous revela-tions, many of your contacts may be shocked or startled. They will not immediately know how to take the new you. And what happens if you begin to show some of the stored-up anger you have against your parents to people who know them? Stories might get back to your parents, and hurt them.

Your parents themselves are a particular problem. The parts of you which you most need to change are the bits they taught you through pain. You now have to reject these lies. On the whole, however, it does not seem to be a good idea, if they are still alive, to phone them up one night and tell them that you have finally taken over; that you have inside you a child's hatred of them for the casual cruelties they imposed on you; that you do not need any more to rely on their love as you did when you were a child; that their love was conditional anyway, and not good enough. You cannot be blamed for thinking right now that while all this may be necessary in theory, and all very well for those people whose parents really hurt them, in your case it does seem to be going to extremes, and need-lessly hurting people who did their best, and who love you.

There are very few people who, when they start to learn how to change, do not come up against such ob-stacles. The people you share your life with have got used to treating you a certain way. They have encouraged you to not-change. Some will not take kindly to you becoming your own person. They will show that you are hurting them by swallowing all this psychological nonsense and tell you that your actions are selfish and ungrateful, and perhaps a little crazy. And one way or another, through words or actions, they are quite likely to make it crystal clear to you that the feelings you really have are not the ones they want you to have. Gently or angrily they will try to insist that you feel what they want you to feel, that you have a duty to alter your ways to suit them, not to please yourself.

Replacement parents

How do you get round this obstacle? Can you recognize it for what it really is? That feeling of being up against the impossible is the old familiar impossible demand rearing its head yet again. Over the years you have carefully selected people to share your life with who are to some extent replacement parents. They know how to plug into your weak areas. They can, if they wish, avoid talking to you altogether, and simply address themselves directly to the parent in your head. Because they are partly there as a substitute for your parents, they know what makes you feel guilty, or angry, worried or afraid. The people you are close to are by definition those who have the most power to hurt you emotionally, because they know best, out of all the people in the world, what hurts you and makes you feel bad. They would hardly be friends, lovers, parents or children if they did not know you well enough for this. Maybe they do not do this deliberately, but they have the power to do it. And you let them have this power.

Wives and husbands are nearly always replacement parents to some extent; many of them are almost complete replacements. The traditional way of growing up, getting married, and settling down is to choose a girl like mum, or a boy like dad. In the majority of families, when a child grows up and gets married, he or she tries to choose somebody the parents will approve of. Somebody like themselves, or near enough like themselves to be able to do a similar job of looking after their child. People very rarely marry somebody from a different class, or with a different standard of education. Most people marry from their own neighbourhood. Also, we tend to fall in love and to marry people whom we see as very similar to ourselves in tastes, opinions, outlook on life, attitudes. With almost unerring instinct we look out for and find a person who has been brought up to understand us, because he or she has been subjected to a similar process of up-bringing. We find a person who can plug into the parent in our head and take over from it to help us do the job at that time we are innocently trying to do ourselves, namely to take over where our parents left off.

Our friends are the people we trust most. But what does this mean? Usually it means that we know they can hurt us, but prefer not to. We chose them because they seem to understand us. They are usually people who have a similar set of impossible demands from their parents that they are trying to meet. We give them the power to make us feel guilty, to press the same buttons which our own parents can press, and which our parents put there. That is why we feel at home with our friends.

If you have children of your own, then it is as well to face the fact that they have made a life-time study of you and your personality. They know what makes you angry, and afraid; what makes you worry and stops you being decisive. They can place impossible demands on you too, by triggering off any of these reactions. You have given them this power; it is part of the way you have loved them. In this way even your children become to some extent substitute parents. If you doubt this still, consider when it was that one of your children last noticed you feeling tired, and volunteered, unasked, to do some small chore for you, such as the shopping, cooking, or washing up.

If this happens quite often, you are probably pleased. If not, you are probably indignant. Parents expect their children to look after them from time to time. They expect their own children to act in a parental way towards them. They encourage it. So they should not be surprised at the idea that their children can be substitute parents.

The power struggle

So what happens when you start to change? Your wife or husband, your friends and children, your neighbours and colleagues may accept the new you without question. But if they do put up any resistance, this is because you are threatening them. And the part you are threatening is the power they have over you as substitute parents. If you let them keep this power you are helping them to preserve your tendency to have breakdowns.

You cannot afford any longer to let them have this power. So you have to take it away from them as gently and as firmly as possible. What you have to be able to do is to stop over-reacting whenever they make you feel like a child again, faced with an impossible demand. In other words, if one of these people says something to you in such a way that you feel like a threatened child, you have to stay calm and refuse to feel trapped. Remember that at that moment you have two reasons for feeling threatened. One reason is to do with the immediate circumstances. The other is to do with the way you were treated as a child. It is alright to use the anger which stems from the immediate circumstances. But not to use the childhood reservoir of anger and fear. If you feel angry, say so in a calm, adult voice. Explain also that you feel threatened, as if you were a child again. Do not put the blame for this on the other person, but say that this is a problem you always have when you are spoken to like that, and admit that you are concerned about this reaction and trying to get rid of it. It does not matter if the other person fails to understand. What is more important is that you get through the crisis without connecting up the two sets of feelings—your immediate ones, and your childhood ones. It is important not to apologize for this. Beware particularly of saying, 'I'm sorry, but ...'. You have nothing to be sorry for. And these words do not really mean you are sorry in any case. They really mean 'I am angry or afraid, and ...'.

Talking to your partner

A closer look at the examples mentioned earlier should help you get a better understanding of the tactics you need. Suppose you are married, not happy about some aspect of sex with your partner, and that over the years you have kept more and more of this feeling hidden. How do you stop hiding your feelings?

First, of course, you have to be honest with yourself, and face up to any anger you have with your parents at the way they left you ill-equipped to show sexual feelings. You have to do this by yourself. Then you have to be quite certain that you really want to take full responsibility for how you feel, and for being honest with other people. Only when you have done this will you be truly ready to open up the problem, and to tell your partner how you feel. What you do next is to choose the right time to talk about sex. Some people find that after sex is best; others that it is best to choose a casual moment of relaxation which might, with the right moves lead to sex. You know your partner best, and only you can decide. But find the time when your partner is likely to talk, and not likely to feel threatened. Then say that over the years you have been afraid of hurting your partner's feelings. This was because you had been brought up to feel guilty about sex. You now want to say something which you feel strongly, and that has to be faced by both of you. You want a more honest relationship in which sex is more fun, and where talking about sex so you can both be happier becomes a natural part of the relationship.

If your partner over-reacts, stay calm. Let it happen, without feeling guilty or threatened. Remember that over-reaction can take two forms—your partner might feel criticized and get angry, or go very quiet and ignore what you said. Say what you really feel, and leave it at that. Your partner might, of course, also read this book, and recognize that he or she also has a parent-in-the-head to deal with. You deal with yours. Let your partner deal with his or hers. Taking responsibility for your own life is safest if you do not take responsibility for your partner's life. The main tactical points are to reduce the threat to yourself from your own parent-in-the-head, and to give your partner a chance to do the same for himself or herself. Stay calm. Use an adult voice, not a child voice or a parental one. Make no threats. Try to communicate, but if your partner won't, leave it. If the problem is complicated, for example if you have had a lover your partner is unaware of, or your partner may have had one, then do not try to do everything at once. The main objective is not to hurt one another, but to learn again how to treat each other as free adults. If you no longer find your partner sexually attractive, or do not love your partner, then decide for yourself whether you want to stay with him or her before you open up the subject: this is part of taking full responsibility for how you feel. Above all, keep your head-parent out of it. He or she will only make trouble.

Talking to your children

Consider next the problem of child-parent breakdowns in communication. This is an equally vast subject, and all you can do here is get an idea of the principles involved, and work out the rest for yourself. The first two steps are the same: being honest with yourself, and getting rid of as much anger and fear from the childhood reservoir as you can before you re-open communication with the other person. Next, choose your moment, preferably one where the child concerned is relaxed and you are relaxed. Say that you want your child to understand that you love him, *and* that you do not like some of the things he does. This is because they frighten you, and make you angry. (Do not say you love him *but* ... This means you only love him if he behaves your preferred way.) You have now decided that being frightened and angry are your own problem, not the child's. So you are no longer open to blackmail. Say that you will continue to trust him, and to feel angry if this trust is broken. But what he does will no longer threaten you in future, because it will be the child's problem, and you have decided not to make it one of your problems any longer. Again, if the child over-reacts, let him. Stay calm, and do not connect up with your own deep anger. The responsibility for what he does is his. You cannot expect to be a perfect parent; nor to have a perfect child. If the parent-in-your-head says this is wrong, point out to him that he did no better than you are doing, and tell him to get lost.

You may be in a difficult position because the child already has too much built-in anger towards you, and too much fear of you, to be able to cope with it. This too has to be faced, but not all at once. Remember that your child will only be free to deal with this anger and fear when he reaches the age to separate from you and live away from home. His feelings are his problem, and he has the right to choose his own time for dealing with them. Your child is already an individual in his or her own right. All the rights which you have taken for yourself apply equally to your children. The best you can do

94

is to stop directing anger, which should really belong to your parents, at your own children. If you can give your children the right not to like you, and live with this, you will have set yourself and them free.

Talking to your parents

If your parents are alive, you may have to face up to the fact that they would not be able to understand your anger towards them. If they can, and if you can talk over such problems with them, then clearly this will help you enormously. But the real problem is not your present-day living parents, but the parent-in-your-head, the part of you which acts as a trigger for guilt and anger and fear. If your parents always make you feel bad when you meet, stop going to see them, or cut down your visits as far as possible, while you come to terms with your hidden anger. Talk things through with a counsellor, or somebody you love. Work through the anger. If you have to see them and do not get on with them, your parents are best treated with careful indifference. Above all do not get caught up in a row with them. It will only repeat the pattern of your childhood and make you feel worse.

No easy answers

It has to be stressed again that in all these matters there are no easy answers. Ultimately, if the people who surround you will not allow you to exercise your rights, and if you are completely free of childhood anger, then it is best to move on and make new relationships. Staying in bad relationships and making other people happy will only preserve your tendency to have breakdowns. You cannot make somebody happy; nor can anybody else make you happy. All you can do is be happy and share your happiness. Sometimes it is better to accept that a relationship has run its course, and that to keep investing in it will only turn you into a compulsive gambler, an unhappy person who has dedicated his life to losing in the pretence that he will win some day soon. Better to have a broken relationship than a nervous breakdown. You will have more chance of recovery.

Index

97

Overcoming Common Problems Series

The ABC of Eating
Coping with anorexia, bulimia and
compulsive eating
JOY MELVILLE

An A–Z of Alternative Medicine
BRENT Q. HAFEN AND KATHRYN J.
FRANDSEN

Arthritis
Is your suffering really necessary?
DR WILLIAM FOX

Being the Boss
STEPHEN FITZSIMON

Birth Over Thirty
SHEILA KITZINGER

Body Language
How to read others' thoughts by their gestures
ALLAN PEASE

Calm Down
How to cope with frustration and anger
DR PAUL HAUCK

Comfort for Depression
JANET HORWOOD

Common Childhood Illnesses
DR PATRICIA GILBERT

Complete Public Speaker
GILES BRANDRETH

Coping with Depression and Elation
DR PATRICK McKEON

Coping Successfully with Your Child's Asthma
DR PAUL CARSON

**Coping Successfully with Your Child's Skin
Problems**
DR PAUL CARSON

**Coping Successfully with Your Hyperactive
Child**
DR PAUL CARSON

Curing Arthritis Cookbook
MARGARET HILLS

Curing Arthritis – The Drug-free Way
MARGARET HILLS

Curing Illness – The Drug-free Way
MARGARET HILLS

Depression
DR PAUL HAUCK

Divorce and Separation
ANGELA WILLANS

The Epilepsy Handbook
SHELAGH McGOVERN

Everything You Need to Know about Adoption
MAGGIE JONES

**Everything You Need to Know about Contact
Lenses**
DR ROBERT YOUNGSON

**Everything You Need to Know about the
Pill**
WENDY COOPER AND TOM SMITH

Everything You Need to Know about Shingles
DR ROBERT YOUNGSON

Family First Aid and Emergency Handbook
DR ANDREW STANWAY

Feverfew
A traditional herbal remedy for migraine and
arthritis
DR STEWART JOHNSON

Fight Your Phobia and Win
DAVID LEWIS

Flying Without Fear
TESSA DUCKWORTH AND DAVID
MILLER

Goodbye Backache
DR DAVID IMRIE WITH COLLEEN
DIMSON

Good Publicity Guide
REGINALD PEPLOW

Helping Children Cope with Grief
ROSEMARY WELLS

How to Be Your Own Best Friend
DR PAUL HAUCK

How to Control your Drinking
DRS W. MILLER AND R. MUNOZ

Overcoming Common Problems Series

Overcoming Common Problems Series